VOICE OF THE SOUL

VOICE OF THE SOUL

BY

SOREN

CHANNELLED THROUGH

MELSA DOWDELL Minister (Retired)

First Published 2005

This publication is printed on paper derived from sustainable forests. The cover is made from recycled material.

ISBN 1 899750 282

Printed in Great Britain.

A catalogue record for this book is available from the British Library.

Aureus Publishing Limited
Castle Court
Castle-upon-Alun
St. Bride's Major
Vale of Glamorgan
CF32 0TN

Tel: (01656) 880033 Fax: (01656) 880033
Int. tel: +44 1656 880033 Int. fax: +44 1656 880033

E-mail: sales@aureus.co.uk
Web site: www.aureus.co.uk

To Leif Amber, my granddaughter.

I dedicate this book to my granddaughter,
For saving me so many times when I 'crashed the computer!'
Love, courage and blessings on your journey to Wisdom and inner
knowledge.
So be it.

Nan.

ACKNOWLEDGEMENTS

To Maureen Roderick and Joseph Fordham whose loyalty and love, enabled me to complete this book and I thank them for their strength and support.

To Mark Horton – forever the excitable questioner – for his encouragement to persevere with my endeavours and his belief in the work I do.

Also my thanks go to others who were in my group over the years and who are now teachers and workers in their own churches and are still exploring the exciting journey of Spiritual Awareness. Many thanks to Terry and Shirley Murphy of Ebbw Vale and Ineke Ribberling, who has recently left Wales to return to her homeland in Holland, for their support over the years – my love and blessings go with you on your journeys!

Last but not least, many thanks to Andrew Smith, whose support helped finalise Soren's book 'Voice of the Soul.'

VOICE OF THE SOUL

CONTENTS

INTRODUCTION

This is not a book about religion. This is a book which aims to help those on a spiritual path (whatever their affiliations), and also those who have not yet consciously begun their journey. So in some ways this is a guide book, providing helpful directions to encourage and facilitate spiritual travels, whilst giving commentaries on some of the sights, pitfalls and obstacles along the way.

The teachings in *Voice of the Soul* were channelled through an experienced medium, so the actual author of this book is not currently incarnated on this planet. Known to us as Soren, this advanced Soul is one of seven in a group, existing on a higher plane, whose present purpose is to impart teaching to the earthly plane. This mission is mirrored all over the world by similar groups disseminating the same wisdom. We refer to Soren as 'he' merely because he identifies himself with a male name. For since he and his group only exist as energy, they have no specific gender. Although Soren and his group each have separate identities and personalities, they share a collective consciousness which is itself a precursor and indicator of the later stages of man's own evolution.

Soren is very clear that he and his companions are not to be held in awe by those who hear their information, for the knowledge that they impart is already within us, and at some other point in time, we shall be the ones to impart it. Their identities and positions hold no importance for them, for they maintain that their teachings are the overriding aspect of the communication, although Soren has described two of his incarnations and deaths in very moving terms.

Communication with Soren began in May 2002. The method itself is relatively straight forward and well-known: the experienced medium goes into a trance and effectively moves his or her consciousness aside, allowing the higher being to step in and make use of the medium's body in order to communicate with the physical plane. During the channelling the medium has no knowledge of what is being said for (in this particular case) she can only hear the voice of the channelled spirit, not those of the others in the room. For the inexperienced this is a relatively dangerous activity, and even for experienced mediums the high vibrations make this both a physically and mentally exhausting effort. For this reason each session usually lasted no longer than 50 minutes.

Our group initially consisted of Melsa Dowdell, a well-known and respected medium; Joseph Fordham, and Maureen Roderick, who are both practising healers and rostrum workers; and Mark Horton, who although he had no previous experience of group work, is well versed in spiritual teaching and literature. The aim of our group was to work on spirit communication, and not to receive teachings and wisdom. However the continued insistence of Soren to be present at our meetings convinced us of this different aim. After a few sessions we began recording everything that was said, both for a record and also to help to understand what was being taught to us. It was only later, when the extent and value of the channelled teachings became apparent, that the idea of publishing the transcripts came to light.

Each chapter in *Voice of the Soul* consists of one of Soren's teaching sessions, sometimes framed by questions before and after. It was remarkable how many times the pre-planned questions were answered without being asked, and the familiarity of the meeting's participants often resulted in jovial banter between planes of existence.

Soren's teachings are simple yet profound. He teaches that through knowing the self in a true sense, the realisation that we are Soul in physical form can be apparent to all, and with this conscious union of man and Soul, this journey can rapidly move on.

SOREN'S INTRODUCTION

A short time after the completion of the book it was suggested by the group that it would be an advantage if Soren gave a short introduction to its contents and why it would benefit people to read it.

We met as usual, but with a guest, Andrew Smith, who had been proof-reading the transcripts and had also been present for some of Soren's lessons. We sat quietly waiting for Soren to join us, and after a short period he came through with the following:

"It gives us pleasure to be with you once again. But this will only be for a short time and we thank you for inviting us to speak about the book on which you have all worked so hard. If it were not for people such as yourselves we of Spirit would not be able to communicate with you to bring forth that knowledge which man needs to gain the wisdom that dwells within his being, for unless man endeavours to persevere towards his Soul's desire he cannot become one with Self.

My friends and I have come to this small dedicated group with the understanding that they wish to grow, that they wish to become one with the true Self which dwells within, to identify themselves with those who have gone before and with those who have reached an aim in life and continued their journeys in other dimensions, and yet many of those have returned to the Earth plane so they may grow in worldly experience to benefit – *not* the Soul – but *man*, for it is *man* who must evolve – the Soul already *is*!

We would ask those of you who read this book to understand the need to undertake the inward journey which is to reach that place of Stillness and Silence and which is of great importance, where you may become one with the true Self. It is hoped that as your measured time on Earth passes, you will begin to understand that time in itself is of no value, and if it be that during *this* lifetime you do not wish to seek Self then be it so, but we tell you there are many of your world who in seeking Self have reached only the borders of Self and are on the verge of becoming One and in so doing, the One which they seek will be identified as the True Master Soul. The Master Soul in itself is identified with the Great Spirit – is identified with that which you call God.

If one sits and waits, when the time is right the teachers will approach. It is said 'God helps those who help themselves', and this is true, for in helping yourselves to discipline your minds and go deeper into your meditations you will find so much help given to you which will assist you on your path of spiritual awareness.

When we speak of stillness it is stillness of the mind, and when we speak of silence it is the silence of the mind that you should be seeking, for within that stillness and silence is man's true identity.

When we speak of Divine Love and True Compassion we mean those qualities which are within man and yet they are balanced with fear and hate, with jealousies and this is the sadness of it all, for as man grows he is very often unaware that that which will attack him from outside of Self causes *him* to allow the turmoil he suffers by allowing such happenings to be. So therefore, school yourselves to be still which will enable you to ward off pain and anger inflicted by others, for it is not your pain, it is not your anger unless the conscious mind wills it so, and man must then start again at the beginning of his search whereby he will need to reinstate himself in the Stillness and Silence of his being.

It is hoped that you the reader, will benefit from the teachings we have brought and yet in truth these teachings are already known to you. In the rush of your world you know you should find time to be still and yet you disregard the still small voice that says to you – Be still and know that I AM there!

Within each and everyone dwells this I AM, but man in his haste to progress, whether it is of a material desire or that of the Spirit, refers to that I AM as the personal identity of himself and this is not so. Man is simply a commodity through which Spirit works, albeit with a thinking mind and emotions, but in which the little Soul resides. Man has been created for one purpose only, and that is to allow the Soul in its knowledge – in its wisdom – in the desire to manifest God on this plane and others through the physical being of man. But the Soul also wishes to seek within the mind of man to bring forth that knowledge and wisdom into his *conscious* mind, enabling him to become one with God and Self.

1

WISDOM

A question was asked about wisdom.

"You ask of wisdom. There are many ways in which to gain knowledge. From books, from others who seemingly are to you further along the path of spiritual understanding, and yet man lacks the ability to understand the knowledge he has gleaned from these other ways and instead he creates his own understanding. It is not until man gives himself completely to the heart of his being will he gain the wisdom that he so greatly desires.

Wisdom consists of free thinking.
Wisdom consists of free exploration.
Wisdom consists of the Soul within you expressing itself.

Your desire for wisdom is greater than your desire for true spiritual knowledge. For once you have gained true spiritual knowledge, wisdom is an automatic reaction. For it is through knowledge of the Spirit and the Self, and the Soul that dwells within the physical heart of man, that wisdom lies. It has been said, 'The heart is the home of Wisdom and in the depth of the mind of man is this knowledge.'

One can read books by great masters which contain much knowledge, but you are your own master – you are your own teacher, and if you choose to step into that place of Stillness, Wisdom will open itself to you. She is one that walks with you. She is one that is part of you and the Soul that is progressing in whatever form it chooses to. That Wisdom is with that Soul, for the Soul is part of the divine master, the one you call God.

It is wise to admit that even the most advanced one amongst your people can say 'I know nothing', for in truth, man knows nothing. It is through his seeking for wisdom and allowing himself to draw in that wisdom to his conscious mind that he becomes wise; he becomes one with his true Soul-Self.

1

What is Wisdom?
Wisdom is that great understanding and knowledge of truth.
What is Truth?
Truth is that great understanding of Soul expression.
It is the great manifestation of Wisdom, the sister of that you call
God, for she and he, it or that, are one.

The quality of the God-Self is in man's being. It is part of man's consciousness and yet man remains unconscious of this knowledge. For to man knowledge comes in the spoken and written word, but true wisdom can not be expressed in these forms. True wisdom is the movement of the Soul as it manifests its Self through the human form and the act of that human form is Wisdom.

We can put together many words to express the way of Spirit and of God, but in the inner mind of man this is already known, for it is God that dwells within that inner mind.

Open the door of your heart in a conscious effort and the 'Book of Wisdom' will be opened. And as you familiarise yourselves with these wise words, you will realise that you already know this truth, for it is the God within you recognising the truth within you as being that truth of Himself – of your Self – that expression of God which you term the Soul.

What is it we expect from gaining Wisdom?

Wisdom is already there! The conscious mind in its effort to join within the heart of Wisdom becomes wise in its action that manifests into your world. For that which you give will be compassion in the heart of Wisdom.

What does Wisdom consist of?

It is not just knowledge, it is the truth of God expressing God, and man's wisdom in understanding this knowledge is realising that aspect of his Soul is God.

Wisdom in itself is without words. It is a Knowing. It is knowing that the steps you have taken along your path was the path of the individual God-Soul returning to the Source of God – wherein All Wisdom lies.

What do we mean by All Wisdom? Is it greater than Wisdom itself?

It consists of all that is beautiful in thought, word and deed, but mostly of thought. For thought is impressed on the conscious mind of man by the Soul that dwells within. You may say some thoughts are evil. This is because the Soul has become misguided and attracted to the earthly pleasures and gains. In itself it is not evil. Evil only exists in the heart of man's physical being and the thoughts he himself expresses and desires. If you allow the Soul to express its true Self, it can only express wisdom, love, compassion and the quality you refer to as God. For it is God expression from the Soul of man which is the part of God, which is God. If man can understand this then he will have taken a large step into the unknown world of Wisdom.

Man lacks wisdom for he has not allowed the conscious mind to turn the key to the heart which contains wisdom. It may well be, as you listen to another expressing his understanding and expression of wisdom, that you are attracted by his way of seeking, but if his seeking is not on the path of total stillness and silence in the physical mind and the emotional state of his being and physical neglect, then wisdom will become unattainable.

What do we mean by this?

It is for you to search in truth – your true desire, while you are walking this plane in physical form as the progressing Soul, to understand that it is the Soul, first and foremost, which is the important thing in the conscious, physical life. For without this Soul influence man cannot be. Man must open to the wisdom that dwells within him, but with the knowledge that if he begins to understand – just a little – his true destiny lies in Spiritual Wisdom of the Law of God and not of man, and then his journey will be a joyous one. All that joy expression will become manifest in his physical being, his heart and his mind.

Will this then mean there will be an end of suffering?

No, it does not mean this. It simply means initially the Soul is allowed, through the co-operation of man, to express its wisdom, its divinity, through the conscious mind.

Man himself will be at peace.
Man himself will be filled with joy.

Man himself will disregard any ailment that may attack his body, for his Soul is free and this freedom can separate itself from any physical form of pain and sorrow. Pain becomes nothing: for the mind of man is filled with joy and his realisation that he is one with Spirit and one with God, and Wisdom has been opened to sit in the mind of man and he is a Christ Being who walks this earthly plane. When he returns to the place of Spirit it will not be at the level that is similar to your earthly realm, but will return to a place of yet greater wisdom. All is in the Soul of man, for the God, the creator of all things, has deemed it so!

All qualities of God are within man's being. God is love and 'love is sufficient unto Itself' and love returns to itself in the form of the conscious mind of man. And when man realises this, he will become - in truth - one with the Christ Consciousness and his Buddhic Nature and the Wisdom of that which you call God."

"Do you understand?"

Those present agreed they did and voiced their appreciation for the enlightened talk given that evening.

2

FUSION OF THE SOUL

Mark voiced the question of fusion with one's Soul and how this could be accomplished. He also asked if the one speaking would identify himself with a name by which the group could address him.

"Man's mind is filled with questions and even though all answers are within his being he is reluctant to listen to the silence and the voice that speaks in that silence.

When man begins his journey on this Earth he is a grown Soul – he simply dwells in the small form of the physical babe, but the Soul itself is in an advanced stage of progression. It is the little mind of man that asks the questions and it is the advanced Soul which dwells within that give the answers.

If man in his commitment to spiritual growth could only understand that the aim of the Soul is to simply bring forth that manifestation of God impression on to an earthly level, thereby bringing the God-Self into focus of man's own mind and the mind of others. If the God-wisdom was available to each and everyone on your Earth level, your world would be as you have termed in the past 'The Garden of Eden', in which all is beautiful – that which you see and feel, hear and know; but because of the limitation within the mind of man who has not listened to his Heart-Self and the Soul voice that dwells within, this God-wisdom cannot be! It may be that you will ask – 'How can God not be, when he is over all that is living and all that he has created?' Man can prevent the power of God coming into this world by simply using that which you term *FREE WILL! God's Gift to the physical being.*

It is not the Soul itself that has free will. The Soul is dedicated on the path of God-wisdom to manifest in physical form. *That* is its desire – *That* is its God-Self expression.

Man has free will. Man has been given a mind with which to investigate, to create, to destroy, to keep still, and it is only in the stillness of man's mind that the God-Self can manifest. The

Soul is on a path of progression, and progression is the state of bringing the God-Self to Earth. That is its aim! Man can unite with the thought that is being imprinted in the mind: to go within to seek the knowledge and the wisdom that he so desires. Man claims to understand this and sits in his meditative state and enters the Silence, not knowing what true silence is. He enters the stillness not knowing what true stillness is. It is not simply an end of movement or an end of noise, for within the silence there are the thought impressions that will guide the conscious mind of man to its Soul-Self – its true identity! In the stillness is the action of movement – of Soul vibration as it enters the physical surrounding area of that which you call the aura. The aura of man is as dense as the material world. It is as dense as the physical body of man. Albeit, one may see light coming from another, but it does not mean that other has evolved to that degree of spiritual wisdom. At least not in a conscious state, despite the intelligence with which he was born! It simply indicated the possibility of reaching that level while in a physical form in this life time. The soul itself is already evolved to that degree, for it is an aspect of God. It simply indicates the possibility of that man reaching that level while in the physical form. It is the strength of the Soul that radiates this light and colours. You may say at this point, 'Then why the need of a physical body if none of these qualities are within the physical mind and heart of man?' But these qualities *are* there, they lie dormant, and they are dormant because man desires that his physical wants and needs are fulfilled first and foremost.

If the Soul is allowed to manifest through the inner being of man, then that which you term God, that which you term Spirit, that which you term Soul, would be at one with the form of man and all the brilliance that you see surrounding one another would be the true light of man, as with the Christ within the physical form of the man, Jesus. Jesus in himself, was - and I repeat, *was*, only a man. The Christ consciousness of which you speak, dwells within each and every man, woman and child before and since the man, Jesus. The difference is that the man Jesus, in his devotion to his father God, as he is referred to, reached a stage of true open awareness of his own identity as a physical being, that he had the power to deny or allow the Christ consciousness to become alive within his physical form and actions.

This is all for you. The form in which you live is not of such great importance that the fear of death should deny you the true awareness of what you are and why you are here. As you use the implements of your world to create, so too is the Soul that dwells within using the physical form to create that which it wishes.

I say, 'which it wishes', for the Soul, if it has become absorbed by material desires, will create only that which satisfies itself, for its path has been darkened by the free will of man. In so saying this, it does not mean that the Soul's progression will end, for it cannot end, for it has never began in the sense that man might understand, it has always been! That aspect of God has always been within man! It does not end – it does not begin. It is that which was, which is, and evermore will be!

You measure your lifespan with time, and time in itself is not of any importance to the Soul part of you. It is a measurement of wisdom within the Soul understanding and it is through this understanding that the Soul expression can become one with the mind of man. The Soul, if it is allowed to express its own true wisdom of God, then the free will of man, in a conscious state, becomes submissive to the Christ Soul within and man's journey becomes filled with expectation without fear, of the knowledge that is available to the conscious mind.

The question that most men and women ask is 'why me?' and the answer usually given is 'why not?' If on your path the sorrows and the pain become unbearable, understand it was a Soul choice. It was a path which that portion, that segment, that aspect of God, has decided to walk in Soul physical form. It may well be that you may say, 'But it is not my Soul – my God-Self, or the Spirit that God has given to me that suffers, it is me – my physical body and mind that feels this pain!' If you deny your free will in true acceptance of what you term to be the will of God, the will of Spirit, the will of the Soul which is One, then you would be joyous as each obstacle in your life presented itself to you and you overcame it, for full co-operation with Soul-Self shows the physical mind the strength that dwells within, the power of its Soul-Self, Man's Soul-Self!

It may be difficult for you as man or woman to understand when pain is afflicted on your loved ones, but understand that the Soul of your loved one has chosen this path for whatever reason. You suffer the pain of that Soul, in human form. That Soul does not suffer in the way of man. The Soul, if it is denied by the anger in man's mind and heart, will simply be still within that being. It does not become disturbed. God cannot be disturbed. It does not become anxious. God cannot become anxious or impatient or angry. Time has no significance to the Spirit-Soul of God. Time was created by man, for man's convenience. The seasons of your world are because of the activity that surrounds it. One universe affects another. The *measurement* of time and season is dictated by man.

When we speak of time we use it in a way for you to understand that it is not time passing, but you passing *through* that element of time. And as you pass through and you acknowledge your true Soul-Self, the Soul becomes stronger in its own identity, which is God, and this is transmitted to the mind of man who recognises what he is, why he is here and what his purpose is in life. His purpose is to walk the earthly plane in all its glory, and its ugliness that man has created, to allow the beauty of God to manifest and reflect back into this world and in the form of man. The aura that you would see around your brothers and sisters at this point would be greater – would be immense and your world would light with the light within man - the light of Spirit, the light of God and the light of the little Soul.

The questions men ask God are always of personal gratification, whether it be of a material nature or a spiritual nature. In so doing he has separated himself from that God being because of his physical mind. The questions that he prepares affect the Soul's response, because man himself is a selfish being. If the Soul-Self was allowed to manifest as the Spirit-God-Self these questions would not arise, for man would already know the answers. In so happening, the torment of the questions in man's mind would become still and as nothing, and man would find peace on Earth and peace in his heart, thus allowing true Soul expression. Therefore the greatest challenge of the God-Spirit-Soul Self is to become one with its own creation, thereby expressing God-Self as a WHOLE.

When you bring a child into your world it is hoped that child will be healthy, will do well in life, and will prosper. What are you wishing for this child? Are you wishing for its natural Soul expression to be allowed to evolve, or are you wishing for the physical babe you hold in your arms – albeit a beautiful thing, but that beautiful child has been created to manifest the God-Spirit-Self. Nurture its Soul as you nurture its body. Encourage its Soul manifestation as you encourage its intellect. Bring health to the Soul-Self by loving the soul that dwells within as you would bring health to the physical form. There are many aspects of the physical body of man, his mind and his way, but these aspects are minute in comparison to the greatness of his true being. Man is God made manifest, but this God made manifest is limited by man's reluctance to become as the 'drop of rain in the ocean', for he is afraid of losing his identity with which he is familiar. If man is familiar with his Soul-Self then the question would now be '*How can I allow this manifestation of God?*' You would not lose your individuality of being the God within because you are one with that Divine individual. You would lose, and willingly so, that identity you associate with physical character and worldly gains. As you grow in spiritual understanding you will realise the earthly gains are as nothing in comparison to the conscious awareness of inner peace, inner love, and inner healing; and that inner peace, inner love, and inner healing will be made manifest in your world and its people. You will recognise the God whom you place in a different sphere to yourself as being on the same sphere which covers all spheres of creation.

The spiritual path is a difficult one, for man is reluctant to be at one with himself. He in physical form is dissatisfied with himself, with his life, even with those he loves, for he cannot see his own reflection on this world. He sees the destruction, but that is placed on the shoulders of God – he is blamed! Man will accept responsibility of the glorious events of his world, but if he allows himself, as man, to become true Self, as Soul, then he would understand not only inner peace, but human peace and worldly peace, and would also recognise that all is one!

Mankind cannot progress all at once for it would create great pain upon those that are not even seeking the light within the Soul. Such a transformation would be of no benefit to the progressing Soul for its work in trying to manifest the true God-Soul would not be fulfilled if man himself was transformed without conscious awareness. It is for the God-Spirit-Soul-Self to create this transformation with the co-operation of the conscious mind, slowly and gently awakening man to his true potential. There are those among you who have already stepped upon this path of transformation and their journey has taken many lifetimes, but they are filled with the understanding that each lifetime was one progressive step towards true realisation and God manifestation.

When a question arises during your times of quiet meditation, ask it first of your Soul-Self, which is God – of the Spirit that dwells within, which is God - and of that which you call God - and you will be guided by an answer which you will know to be TRUE!"

"Do you understand and is there a question you would like to ask?"

To which Mark remarked that the entity had not given them a name by which they could identify the speaker, and he was impressed that it might be a Magi and he asked if this was true?

Our visitor replied, "This one through whom I speak was told of me a long time ago, and for identification I am Soren."

Mark then went on to ask Soren if he could give an explanation of the term expressed as 'The Blazing Fire', to which Soren replied:

"You mean the blazing Light. When man speaks of the Blazing Light there are many variants of these words, but in this case Light is a *knowing*! It is with the brilliance of this light when the understanding of the way of the Spirit impresses itself upon the mind of man and all becomes clear. It is as you would say in your world – 'Eureka', or 'I have seen the light'. It is simply an expression of understanding and it comes suddenly and you are in that Blazing Light. You have grown spiritually but in a conscious awareness as it is meant to be."

"Do you understand?"

Joseph thanked Soren on behalf of the group for his talk that evening, adding that they were already looking forward to their next meeting and wished Soren and his friends goodnight until then.

3

MANIFESTATION

"Everything is in a state of manifestation. Every movement, every action from man, from your Earth, from the universe which surrounds your little world, is in a state of manifestation. Even what you *think* is an expression of manifestation.

Or would you prefer to know the manifestation of Spirit? If it is, then that which manifests is the Soul identity of the physical being. If you mean of the true Self, it is an action made manifest and is that which has been created by the one you call God. You have all come from a source of True Divinity.

Manifestation of the Spirit is in all forms of life and yet you separate and divide and terminate the ability of Soul manifestation by your physical mind, by your need to dissect information that we from the world of Spirit, offer you. When we say 'the world of Spirit' we are *also* creating a division from that one source from which we all come. There is no manifestation of Spirit on your physical Earth: it is the natural movement of Spirit and Soul development. *It is that which is! You* are manifestations of your true Self – your Soul-Self. Your Soul-Self is the manifestation of the Spirit-Self. Your Spirit-Self is the manifestation of the God whom you worship and yet in your fear you neglect to worship the divine within!

When you communicate with your Higher Self, the Soul and the Spirit of the masters who approach you, you separate yourself from your Soul as you cannot identify your two selves as being *one*. You place your thinking process in the form of words and the terminology of man is so limited. If you could communicate with us with the power of the mind, the information you would receive would exceed the knowledge of a language. It would become a *knowing.* A knowing in itself is manifestation of Wisdom! The fusion of the mind, which consists of a communication between Soul-Self and man's mental ability, becomes one in itself and in so being all Wisdom that lies within becomes the utmost impression of knowledge one can receive from one's Soul-Self.

If man could be at one with his true Self, the manifestation of true spiritual effort would project itself onto the mind of others. In so doing, the manifestation which dwells within each and everyone would rise to the surface of man's conscious being. This in itself would create the change within the vibration in the physical being of man and the true self of man would be manifested in Soul expression. There would be physical changes in man that others could see. On seeing these changes, the reaction from others would be that of disturbance because the changes that occurred would happen immediately, to the effect that the light radiated from the manifestation of the true Soul-Self projecting itself through the physical form, would create in the observer an element of fear. Once the element of fear has established itself in the mind and the heart of the onlooker, the vibrations created would disturb that Soul manifesting, to the degree that it would cause damage. Not to the Soul, but to the physical being of the one being used as a channel. You have known in the past of mediums that have brought forth the manifestation of a Self being to stand alongside. The disturbance created by shock, by fear, by disbelief has caused injury to the various mediums of the past. The Soul, in recognition that the manifestation and vibration was Soul Appearance, has learned to decrease to a degree, the vibrations and physical alterations. In doing this, the procedure of their manifestation is more gently premeditated, but in the projection the situation around the medium must be of peace and with a gentle nature and with ones who are willing to accept whatever they see. When we say whatever they see, it is because sometimes the Soul projection from the physical body can be disturbing to observe, because the intensity and the speed at which the vibrating Auric Field changes can cause disfigurement of the form. Not of a permanent nature, but until the vibrations become established.

If man wishes to learn how to allow the Soul manifestation of his true Self through the physical form, he must be prepared to become so disciplined that his own thoughts do not interfere. *How can this be done?* This can only be reached when the level of man's conscious awareness of the vibrations in which he works has been attained. It takes discipline and practice. There are those amongst you who are termed as 'naturals': those that have the ability to project the Soul-Self, but this is very, very rare. It usually occurs with those who practice the art of discipline on a daily basis, of total elimination of all thought from the mind. This is not impossible but is extremely difficult, for in the conscious mind of man lies a darker side through which he can become disturbed by that which does not exist, but is of his own creation: fear and the ability in a fearful state of mind to create that which is disturbing to himself and others. It is what you could term the horror of manifestation – a fear in form – be it what it may!

It is a difficult subject to deal with in depth to be clearly understood. It is a subject in which most beings would prefer not to become involved. For true manifestation of beauty of the Soul that dwells within man has a fearful impression in the conscious mind, for man fears what he will see. He hopes that which is expressed in the manifestation he has allowed will be of beauty, but he fears it will be that which hides his darker side.

If you can understand and truly believe that all that is pure Soul and pure Spirit is the essence of God, you in truth, beyond the beauty of your own understanding, then this is what you will express. But if your conscious mind has cast a shadow of fear and allowed that fear to become one with the vibrations that are yours, for Soul manifestation that Soul-Self will appear to be ugly, disfigured, deformed and not pleasing to the eye of the observer. The reaction then of the observer would create a disturbance that would interfere with the Soul's vibrating field, causing further anguish in the Auric Field of man and the impression of that disturbance would imprint itself on the mind of man. The results could be disastrous!

When you speak of manifestation, do you realise that a simple poem that you write indicates the greatness that is within you, for within that small poem miracles of the creation of man are in the process. That which you are is a manifestation, a creation of your Soul-Self. It has become manifest so the Soul can continue its journey of progression – not evolving – not a growing of Soul wisdom, for it is already evolved. It is already wise. Its journey is in encouraging the progression within man's mind to manifest the beauty of Soul-Spirit-God!

If your desire is to manifest that which you are, then consider the road upon which you walk. Is it a journey of self-seeking of your conscious mind, or is it a hunger to simply see a manifestation of the Soul? It is at first wise of you to understand the mechanics of your own mind, as was said before it can create a horror and it can create beauty. If you understand you are, as a physical being, a creation of your Soul-Self and perfect in its creation, then that which you manifest must be of beauty - must be perfection. Think carefully on what you perceive to be manifestation. Do you really want this manifestation; and think carefully what you deem to be manifestation. That which you think is what you will create. The physical being of man has within itself a mind. The mind is often governed by the events of his world and desires. Once man opens his conscious mind and heart to the blending of the Soul which is perfect in itself, then that which he wishes to manifest will be perfection. It is the element of doubt and fear and mistrust in your own Soul-Self- created physical mind that creates your problems because of your rightful possession – FREEWILL!

If we are speaking of the manifestation of moving objects with the discipline of the mind – with the power of the mind, or levitation of the physical body, then understand that you must also discipline that power and you cannot discipline that power unless you are willing to submit to the Soul control of your physical body. If through ego you decide to create these happenings through the power of your mind, then that which you succeed in will not be perfect. It will be imperfect but with an element of perfection that the Soul influences can have on your conscious mind. But the Soul cannot take full control of the mind unless it is willing to submit to the influence of the Soul-Self. Man does need to understand this.

There is a desire in the mind of man to do all that he can to ease the suffering of his brothers and sisters of his world. It is within the mind of man to bring an understanding of his conscious Self and his needs to the minds of his brothers and sisters, but is it the ego – your own creation – which wishes to impress these other minds? If it is, then it is of no avail to the others of your world and certainly of no avail to you as a conscious being in physical form. It is only of benefit to the physical Self and the impressionable minds of your brothers and sisters, if the true Self is being portrayed - the true Self being your Soul-Self - and if *without* manifestation in a physical sense you can impress the minds around you with the growth of your conscious mind in a spiritual sense, then it will be of benefit.

What part then would Ego have to play?

It would still be active, but as the freewill becomes submissive to the will of God, the Ego becomes submissive to the impressions of the Soul-Self. Ego is a creation of man of his own importance and individuality upon his world. If the Ego did not exist then man would be an exact replica of his brother. There would be no variety in your world. In so saying this, am I saying there is no Ego in the world of Self? No, but the variety in the world of Self consists of a shared understanding in various degrees of the wisdom that dwells within. It is not a self-created wisdom but the wisdom of God that is available to man in his conscious effort to affect an awareness of his own Soul-Self and the Self of Spirit. Each one of you in your world are at varying degrees of spiritual understanding, so too are these varying degrees of spiritual understanding in the world of Self. There are many levels in your world. There are many levels in the world of Self.

You have knowledge of the darker side of Self and yet we say if you allow the Soul-Self to influence you, the conscious being, then what is it you are allowing to manifest through your Self? Are we saying that the Self of the darker side is you, or are we saying that the Self of the darker side is an individual Soul separate from your Self? Is it part of both? The individual Soul that has been influenced by the riches and gains which man desires, also man's pain, and the Soul itself has erred in its choice, then it becomes a darkened Soul. The darkened Soul can be manifested through the mind of the Egoist – as above, so below. As below so above. If you understand this then in a conscious state of stillness you must learn to recognise the vibrations manifesting through yourself. If it is pleasing to your open conscious physical mind and if it is good in every way, for do not forget you are experiencing auric vibrations, then understand that the Soul is the enlightened Soul that approaches. If you feel that the Soul manifestation is from the dark, you in recognising this has helped your own Self to project and manifest the perfection that is within. All scales fall from the eyes of your Soul-Self and it sees its own perfection and brings forth that perfection into you, the conscious being!

If man understood himself he would realise the influence he has on his ability to manifest in the form of truth or darkness. You create the shadows over the sun and in so doing obliterate the beauty of the Soul-Self. The Soul-Self becomes disheartened and its action becomes united with the desires of man, but it is still a perfect form. But the Soul in its projection into the physical body, although it retains all the quality of Spirit and the God-Self, has become weakened by the earthly vibrations and is more attracted to the physical ties of life. This may seem contradictory to what we have been teaching, but is in fact true. This is when the Spirit God, the higher element of the Soul, is then needed by that Soul-Self which is in you. It is as though the two separate minds, the physical and the Soul mind, separate themselves so the Soul mind can communicate with the Spirit of the same Soul. The Spirit being an element of the Divine, which is God. Once the Soul has been guided and influenced by the Spirit-Self, the Soul's strength returns and it is able to continue its journey within the form of man's progression – for the union of man and his Soul to become one, and the manifestation of the Soul-Spirit-God-Self, becomes Divine!"

"Do you understand?"

Soren then said there would be no questions that evening and bid the group goodnight.

4

SOREN

The group wondered who Soren was and what previous lives he had experienced. Would he come again to the physical world? What Astral Level was he now on? Who or what was the group with whom he was associated? It was decided these questions would be asked of Soren this evening.

"You ask who I am. I am everything and yet I am nothing, as so too are you. I am part of everything that has existed, that is existing, and will exist; for there is no division between any form of life, whatever that life may be, and time has no essence to Spirit only to man.

As to my history: my history is that of my brothers around me, to teach you, the children of Earth. We are One and yet we are multiple. There is no separation in what we are. There is only the division you ask of us, thereby we give you a name. As to whether that name belongs to the individual that works with you is of no importance.

You accept the man Jesus was born of this Earth and within him was the Christ Consciousness. You do not question the history of the man Jesus, for in truth the man, Jesus came only once. Within that growing Soul – the small part of God – that exists in each and every one of you, came also the advanced spiritual knowledge. Jesus the man simply drew that knowledge into his conscious mind and recognised his own Divinity. You too are of that same Divinity!

As to have I walked this Earth before? Yes, I have walked this Earth many times, but not in the form which could be presented to you if it were possible this night to manifest the form in which I now dwell and which you may see. There are many forms of life. There is the life of the human and the animal, rock, stone, the sea, the rain and the air of the Earth, for all these things are living forms in the sense of Creation. No form is still within itself. It divides, it unites and it becomes, and so too, does man. The identity of the Soul is that of the Spirit, which is what you call

God, and as these energies join and unite and become one, they come in the form of man. That does not mean that the Spirit itself needs to walk this Earth for it exists in all worlds. It can walk the spaces between worlds, for everything is living in a sense of Soul-man's understanding.

I am part of a Group and it is in the union of this group that I am able to converse with you with the co-operation of a physical being. I have worked with others, others you may know and others you may not know. It is of no importance, but the importance is the message we bring.

I have always been and still am and always will be, as so too, will you! There is no difference between us. What you are, I once was. What I am, you will be, but it will not be in the sense of the individualised person known by the name you now use on this Earth. But it will be as a union of Souls and a union of those who have reached a level of Spiritual Consciousness, and it is that Group with which you will identify yourselves – not as 'I' the personality, but as 'We' – the Group Consciousness. If, and on this occasion it *is* being done, you separate yourself from the group, you become again the individual by the name which you choose to be called. The name I give you is Soren. The name I am known as in our Group of Identified Souls is, and can only be, 'All'! The 'All' consists of those Conscious Beings who have gone before and from whom we draw our knowledge of God.

It is as you grow as individuals that you draw knowledge from your teachers, your masters and your mentors. In truth the majority of your knowledge is drawn from the Soul aspect within your physical form. It is not until you reach a certain level of Spiritual Growth in your conscious mind will those that you term as your masters attach themselves to you in a form of a Group.

We as an individual Group are as close to you as we possibly can be without disturbing too much the vibrations around you, which if they become unduly disturbed would cause anxiety to your mental ability and the part you know as the heart, for it is within the surroundings of your physical body that you term the Auric Field which can create or destroy that which you are! In saying this we are not saying it would be of a physical or spiritual destruction, but it would discourage you from reaching further into your inmost heart and mind to see the teachings of Spirit.

When I last walked your Earth I walked it in the fashion of one afflicted by a disease which you know as leprosy. In the condition of that painful disease is when I became as One with the Group with which I am now associated – that I am part of. I came from no great place or great parentage. The disease came from both my parents and my brothers and we died in a valley. That life itself was of no great importance, but the importance of it was I found that which dwells within me to be magnificent in its beauty and in its fear! I could not understand why my body should be so afflicted and yet my heart so uplifted in the physical disfigurement, but within me was the beauty of God.

I walked this Earth many times as both male and female and my lives were of no great importance to the average person of your world. I conquered nothing myself, my riches were nothing but my Soul-Self within awakening my conscious mind to the beauty of God realisation. But is it so important to know of one's past, when one's past consists of a road to Spiritual growth? Does it matter if the Wisdom and the Knowledge which you have obtained comes from a recognised being, or simply from the teacher that dwells within?

If you study the Self, the Soul aspect, which is a divine Spark of God, then you would see beyond the disfigurement of the human being and see instead the beauty of the Soul. When we speak of disfigurement it is not of your physical appearance, but it is the lack of power and strength within the physical mind to seek *within* yourselves.

Life in itself is most precious, but death in its Glory is victorious. For it is in walking the Earth that you gain within your mind and your conscious awareness, the strength to go forward. When you pass into a level of further understanding of life itself beyond death, the limitations of the mind become nothing, for the mind can be projected to all the corners of the Universe with discipline, with devotion towards the growth of Spiritual Knowledge to the awareness and the richness of God!

You do not ask the history of God! You do not ask the history of Christ! And yet the history of God and Christ which was before the beginning of time grew in its own history of gathering all that is of benefit to the Christ Soul.

The opportunities that were given to the prophets and the wise ones of your world are also there for you. The Christ Consciousness dwells within you for it is placed by that divinity you call God. You do not ask what God is, for no man in truth, has seen God with the physical eye, but has sensed to the limit of his

senses the Beauty of God; and in that Beauty, as man sees with his
inner sight, creates a fear within the conscious mind of man, for in
the Glory of that Blazing Fire of Spiritual Wisdom man is afraid to
look. It is as the fear of the darkened night, and yet on awaking to
the morning light man is at ease with himself and his world. That
in itself is a very small picture of God's Glory, but on stepping
into that Blazing Light of God man becomes one with his own
Glory and recognition of his God-Self, and becomes One with God
and all Creation!

It is for man to become the one to undertake the initial step
on his return home to the Creator. You are still entangled on the
downward path of physical experience and it is only by drawing
this strength within you that you finally become aware of the
greater abilities within you.

Your world has advanced greatly over the last century and
yet man still questions himself and his origins. He does not know
who he is and needs to identify with something, but is reluctant to
identify with that which he is! Man is God and God is man and all
that has been created and all that will be created! The
understanding in your conscious minds relating to the Soul-Self is
beyond your limited imagination, but is not beyond the aspect you
call the Soul, for that aspect recognises itself as *GOD!*

You ask who I am and I would tell you, you know who I
am. I am you. You are me, but I am Soren for identification. We
are of that affinity which is as a bloodline between your fathers
and your sons. The bloodline of Spirit runs through each and every
being on your Planet. The bloodline is that of God. When you look
into the eyes of another what is it you see? Is it the complexity of
the creation of that eye? Or are you looking in depth at the true
realisation of a living Holy Being which dwells within that
physical form?

If you could be physically aware enough to experience the
Auric Field around yourselves blending with one another, you
would become aware also of the power and strength within those
Soul Aura Fields and the intense, but gently absorbing energies
that pass between the Soul conscious aware Beings, which results
in two Souls becoming one, not by the individual Spirit, but by the
Divine Spirit of God. Man chooses to remain within his own Auric
Field and in so doing he feels protected inasmuch as no one else
can interfere with those vibrations. It is an unconscious action in
man. It is a form of a wall of protection that he builds when he is

communicating with another. It is a separation of man without the recognition of his own immortality and in not understanding that if one unites with another in the auric sense of the word you would respond positively to those energies and it would be of benefit to the evolution of man's mind accepting his true nature is that of Spirit. The opened human mind would then not react in the way it does towards another. All barriers would fall and minds would awaken to minds, and communication would be on a thought basis. The imprint of your brothers' words would come to your mind as detailed thought with clarity.

We as a group have already assimilated these energies one to another, and we blend as one Whole, but as we are one Whole we also recognise that division between ourselves and other groups within the Spirit World – other groups who choose to remain singular, and groups that choose to come to Earth to teach. Others choose to come into your world, but as a completed group. The numbers within each group can be a few or many.

This group consists of seven but also we are One because we blend in with each others' Auric Field. We, as One, collate through the mind of this channel to give you that which we know, but our knowledge is also limited. We in our turn sit in the silence of our Soul being to communicate again with Higher Spheres, or more wise and knowledgeable spheres. A good comparison would be: 'To a little frog a big frog is God!', and this is how the mind of man thinks. Those of us who identify with the union of Souls understand there are no 'big frogs' but there are wiser ones and we are one in our identification of Soul progression. I speak of Soul progression and not of evolution in the way you understand, for we are all as wise as our mentors. There is no limitation to the mind of Spirit and the mind of man – all that Spirit knows, so too, does man, but man separates himself from Spirit by assuming that when he passes from this life then wisdom and knowledge and understanding will be awarded to him, but this is not so!

Wisdom comes to man on an earthly plane, but the use of wisdom, the enlightenment of wisdom, the knowledge of wisdom, comes as he grows spiritually and more often than not when he passes *into* the earthly planes! Therefore that which you seek will be found if you are willing to go within the silence of *your own* being. We speak to you with words transmitted through this channel, but in the silence of your being can come, in full, impressions of Wisdom beyond words, but we understand the

necessity of words in your world and we understand the necessity
of the written word in your world, so therefore we come as a
United Group of Souls with a little more understanding of
knowledge than yourselves, and we endeavour to bring you that
same understanding.

If you could experience the state in which we reside you
could not tolerate the vibrations which would enter your own
Auric Field, for they would be as though the very life was being
taken from your physical forms. The vibrations around those of us
on a different level are of such intensity that it would be as though
you were unable to breathe and yet, once acclimatised to these
vibrations you would be mentally and Soul-wise enraptured with
the beauty of these circumstances in which you found yourselves.
The colours which would be presented to you would be beyond
your greatest artist's impressions. The sounds you would hear
would be so much finer and more greatly uplifting than your
earthly music is upon your physical ears in your present life.

The beauty of the Soul which has been guided by the
Wisdom of the Masters and who has taken those teachings into the
physical heart and mind of its physical body, would begin to
understand the necessity of bringing that same teaching to others,
in physical form, to allow the majesty of God to manifest into the
world!

If it were possible to bring our vibration field into the
vicinity of this group, you would experience such a lightness of
heart and mind that you would not feel your physical form
whatsoever. You would be formless. It would be as though you
had left your physical bodies in total awareness of your Soul-Self.
That Soul-Self would integrate within your own group. In so doing
you would identify being one with your group. There would be
instant recognition of brother welcoming brother.

When we speak of closeness between the people of your
world and the closeness between the Soul Environment of your
world, they are so vastly different. If Soul awakening could come
to you *now*, when you pray for your brothers and sisters beyond
the physical form, Soul recognition would be!

When someone in your world dies in tragic circumstances
your heart reaches out to them, but it is *not* your heart which
reaches out, it is your *Soul* reaction to the suffering of that other
Soul in the sense that it has been removed from the physical form
before its time, therefore not fulfilling the journey it intended, so

therefore the Soul would need encouragement to return to the physical form to complete its intended journey. You grieve for your loved ones in physical form when they pass into the world of Spirit and we, in a sense, grieve when a Soul returns to us before its due time, for we understand the loss that small portion of God you call the Soul undergoes.

It is not important who we are, or who I am. It is not important who you are as physical manifestations of your own creation, which is the Soul. What *is* important is your recognition of your own Soul Divinity. When this is understood, you as a physical being relate only to Soul identity and your actions in the physical world are understood by your conscious mind as being your Soul choice, and you accept this Soul choice as your *own*, for you and Soul become one. When man and his Soul become One all identity falls away and you are then an individual being in Soul-physical form. Your individuality is that of Spirit. That of Spirit is the individuality of God. You are One with God. You become not a small group which approach others of your world to teach *them*, you become 'the drop in the ocean'. You become that which you praise. You become God in physical, in Soul form, in Spirit form. You become part of the Whole, for you are All!"

5

AS ABOVE, SO BELOW

The following was based on Mark's question regarding the Buddhist philosophy 'As above, so below', and he asked if Soren could give some insight on this. Reference was also made about people who were sometimes 'bothered' by 'troublesome' Spirits and how was this caused? Another question was asked regarding Soren, on the possibility of his return to the Earth plane and when would this be?

"In the world of Spirit there are many levels. As in your world there are different degrees of intelligence, of ability, of wisdom and of acts of good and evil. As above, so below. In the various levels of Spirit there are those who are governed by the materialistic thoughts and it may seem to you that these thoughts, as they are, should not be in the minds of the Souls that dwell in the world of Spirit, but because we are progressing beings we have the time in which we reflect upon the various levels of our understanding. It may seem to you that those of us that are in the world of Spirit have far greater knowledge and act always in the wisest way when we are governing ourselves and those which we use, but this is not always so. When a Soul returns to the world of Spirit, he has led up until now a life that he remembers which he has spent on the earthly realm, and he is still part of that material world, and in that way of thinking his desire could be, in those early days, to return. It is as if, as you grow in age and responsibilities are thrust upon you in your earthly life, you wish for the time of your childhood when there was no pressure put upon you and the world seemed bright, and so too it is in the world of Spirit. The Soul that has returned to us longs to be back with those he loves, or to those to whom he is attracted – this you know.

This you have been taught and experienced, but because we are able to come closer to the children of the Earth to speak through them with their co-operation, we can teach you the way in which you *can*, if you are dedicated to your life of progression for your Soul-Self, enable you *not* to reside in that level which is closer to the Earth, the world you call the 'Summerland'. The place of which you have been told is very similar to the world in which you dwell, but things there being governed by thought form which in itself creates. 'As above, so below!'

Before you can create, you think of the plan of creation and endeavour in physical form to create that of which you have dreamed. In the world of Spirit, in the beginning the action of the newly returned Soul is very similar. He puts in *physical* Soul effort to create that which he desires. Eventually he learns that with the strength of his mind he can create for himself *immediately* that thought form which can now be projected and become. It is the power of the mind that creates that which you desire, but it is the wisdom of the heart in communication with the mind that enables you to create that which is of benefit, not only to yourself, but others of your world.

In the world of Spirit there are those who long to return to the worldly environment, and in so desiring this can present problems for the physical human being – this you know. When Spirit approaches a being of the Earth and impinges in that which you call the Auric Field to reach to the mind of that one, he is in the powerful position of manipulation. It is you in human form that must use your control to keep still, to be calm, and to instruct the new Spirit that approaches. We of Spirit can be rebellious and as naughty children and also create problems. We may seem to be very wise in our actions and in our words, but there are times within our Soul minds when we too feel lost and discouraged. 'How can this be?' you may ask. Is it because we do not understand our true relationship with God and therefore are weakened by our desires? Is it we do not believe that we are part of God and therefore are unable to be God-like in our actions? There are those among us who believe we *are* greater than God, as so too do the people of your Earth. It may seem strange for one of the Spirit world beings to say such things, but it all rests within the heart of the developing Soul who has experienced physical form.

While the Soul resides in physical form, he is endeavouring to bring that God-like image into the mind of man to manifest that which is of beauty. But when the Soul is at rest in the Spirit world it too suffers from doubt, anxiety and fear, inasmuch as he needs to seek one that will help him and this chain of events continues through all the realms of Spirit. You suffer from doubt, so do we. You in physical form suffer pain and so too, do we. Our pain is lack of Soul strength. The Soul in itself recognises its individuality while in the Soul world, as man recognises his individuality on the Earth plane. Man will seek another to help, the Soul in *its* turn in the Spirit world must *also* seek another. He prays to the God that dwells within, but like you believes that the Spirit that approaches him, to teach and guide, and those that approach you to teach and guide, is revered as a God. It is simply because intelligence is limited in the mind of man he can not envisage God at his greatest, and neither can the Soul that returns envisage that God being as Pure Magnificence.

The children of Earth and the Soul children in the lower realms of Spirit are very similar. If one from the lower realms approaches you it may well be it will be full of mischief and laughter and it could be playful and encourage you also to be playful, but it may not be wise to the degree that it needs to be, to accept the responsibility for its pupil, the man of Earth, and so too, it is on your Earth. As you teach your children the way of right and wrong and you play with your children and stimulate their minds and encourage the powers that are within them – as above so below – the paths of the young Soul in Spirit and the Soul in physical form are almost identical.

In the Spirit world there are also disagreements as groups come together to form one whole, in the sense of completeness among that group. Occasionally there will be a time of disagreement, but because as we begin to search for our group Soul-Self we begin to recognise the level of wisdom and knowledge that dwells within another. We are attracted to that other on a Soul growth level. One seeks one and they seek another and the group grows as in the Earth plane, so too do you seek those friends that you enjoy being with, or that class with whom you will study and learn a particular subject. You become of like minds and it is this way in the world of Spirit. As we grow in the world of Spirit we seek for ourselves as a group, those who are able to expand our own wisdom and knowledge, and these qualities are based on the love that grows, not only within the group, but towards another group, and the love in itself expands – becomes greater – becomes inclusive to a group that was once one or two to numbers far greater; so too, is it on your Earth plane.

As a child enters a school he is singular, but before the end of his learning term he becomes as one with that group in growth and in knowledge and in the times of play and rest. In the world of

Spirit it is the same. Young Souls will gather together to discover, to discuss, to seek, to learn and in their turn seek a teacher among them. That teacher is simply used to express his knowledge and wisdom to that young group of Souls. He is governed in his teachings by one similar to us. He, the young but advanced Soul, is used as we would use a medium of your Earth.

It is not always in the form of teaching and seeking wisdom that the Spirit world is in. There are times when action must be taken to restrain the more excitable Souls. To encourage those who have become weakened, to comfort those who grieve and who wish to return to the earthly plane with their love for another, and the teaching classes become individualised teaching for that particular one Soul. There are some who do not wish to be taught or governed. These are those you refer to as being earth-bound; some for possibly malicious reasons, others purely from grief. But one that approaches you with knowledge and understanding that through you he can enjoy the material returns of your Earth, he is severely reprimanded. *You* turn them to the light; *we* instruct them in the true way of Spirit, in the reasons of the work of Spirit, and encourage and retrain that one to become a lighter Soul in his reaction towards Earth beings. As above, so below!

You imprison and punish those who commit offences in your world but we do not put disobedient Souls in prison or punish them, but we do restrict the power they have to manipulate the physical mind of man. We are able – those of us who are a little more advanced – to put a stop to that power with the power of our own minds. Perhaps it would be easier to explain in a form of mind-control, we are able to lessen the power of the rebellious Soul's ability of mind-control and there is no pain inflicted. There is no limitation to their movements in the level in which they live, they are simply restricted from entering the vibrations of your world. A form of 'imprisonment' without bars! There is no painful punishment given at all. He is re-trained. He is taught to understand the way of the earthly being, and the way of the Spirit being must not cross another's path in the sense that it will cause disturbance to the Earth being. These laws are practised also in your own world. If a child bullies another, you restrict the bully and he is punished in various ways. His actions are limited, his error is pointed out to him so that he cannot inflict his dominance over another, and so it is in the world of Spirit.

As you grow more in the understanding of the gentleness that dwells within you, you are able to manifest that "gentleness" in the approach to your brothers and sisters and you would be looked upon 'as a friend indeed, to a friend in need', with your quiet comfort and your condolences to another who is pained, and so too it is in the world of Spirit. As we grow wiser we grow more powerful, but the power we have is governed by the love that is within and we inflict no pain upon another. We come to guide you, to point you in the right direction, not to control or govern. As in your earthly plane you would not be controlled or governed by another, so too, in the world of Spirit, controlling or governing another Soul would not be from those who are of a higher level.

There are those from Spirit that are often upon your Earth in a form that is not seen by the eyes of man. But in their movement among the people of the world they are influencing one who perhaps shows his anger too quickly, and the Soul who is upon your world without form can impress upon the mind quietness and stillness, and within the heart a gentler nature to be brought forward, so that one who is angry will learn to control his anger. It is also a union of the Soul who approaches and the Soul that dwells within to encourage man's mind to think more gently and lovingly towards his brother. There are three minds in action – the Soul mind that approaches invisible to the eye, the Soul that dwells within that is the life-force to the physical body and the mind of man.

Very often man argues with himself, he could be arguing with his lower nature – that which seeks revenge – or he could be arguing with his higher nature – that which seeks to be at one with his neighbour. It is usually the higher natured side of man which will overcome the lower animalistic nature of man and this is why your world becomes more civilised, or the man of the world becomes more civilised and if it is just one individual who has sought and found that natural element of gentleness and compassion towards his brother, then the Soul within is victorious, and the Soul that has approached to help is also victorious, and man, on understanding that he can control his actions of anger towards another, is also victorious. Three victories which have come about from the union of man's mind, his Soul and an approaching Soul becoming one! So too, is it in the world of Spirit. The troubled Soul without physical form but with the anguish of perhaps the way in which he has lived, or the way in which he now thinks and reacts in the Spirit world, is approached by a Soul friend on his own level who will discuss his pain and who will encourage him to be strong, or perhaps one from another invisible world who is stronger and a more loving and wiser Soul who may approach. A trinity within itself!

The world is a reflection of the heavens above! The heavens above is the mirror that has shone brightly because the Soul has grown in its understanding of that brightness beginning to reflect upon the world of man, and by the world we mean his mind and his heart. It is the endeavour of those of the higher realms that, as man grows in Spiritual and mental wisdom, his world will become as a shining new star that will light the way for others to follow.

As we grow in Spirit we must remember that we are simply humble Souls on the homeward journey to that which we feel is God and our creator. We are returning to the source of life, as so too, are you. We are a little further on our journey. It is a wise Soul indeed, who turns, looks back, and encourages those who follow; and those who follow are wise if they in their turn look back and encourage others on the same journey.

What you are we once were, in different worlds and in different forms, but all consisting of a Soul entity within those different worlds and forms. As we return to the group with which we have great attachment, the joy of our return is shared not only by ourselves, but by those who approach and guide us. As in your world when the black sheep returns to the fold there is much joy if the black sheep has learned his lesson, and so it is in the world of Spirit.

The young Soul is *never* the black sheep! The young Soul has simply become lost for a short period of time and the welcome that he receives will lift him, will strengthen him, will encourage him to go further and seek a higher level of Spiritual growth and in turn he will become the teacher. This path we all walk upon.

You are walking this path now, and the paths in lives before have been in a darker state, but the path in which you walk now is like a candle that glows in a distant future. You can see it, but as yet not close enough to be bathed in its glorious light and that glorious light is Soul manifestation of pure love and beauty. You are beautiful beings simply shaded by the trees of life, but also you need to appreciate the shade, for without it you could not look into the face of beauty. The face of beauty being all that is glorious! As above, so below.

We walk into a brighter and brighter light as we grow, and so too will you!" "Do you understand?"

Thanks were offered by the group, and then Soren invited one question to be asked.

The question asked was: "As a developing Soul have you now, to use a Buddhist expression, broken the wheel of rebirth and you will no longer return to the Earth plane, or will you now go on to a higher plane?"

Soren replied: "I *will* return to the Earth plane. I have dwelt in the world of Spirit for hundreds and hundreds of your years and I have walked with this one (*indicating the medium*) since her birth into the physical plane, but she has not been aware of me, but it does not alter the fact that I have been with her mostly.

When I return to the Earth I will not return alone but I will return with the group in which I am now. It will be many, many years before we return as a united group, when we will be able – and many others will reside in this Earth, who will be able - to communicate with the mind, and although we may be in different parts of your world there will be an attraction of minds and we will be able to instruct and teach each other as we instruct and teach those around us. So too will you, in your turn, become the Spirit teachers of the future and you will have mind communication abilities. You will return to that which is totally natural for the Soul that dwells within. This is the stage where we as a group have reached. We are one in mind and that oneness of mind will remain with us. We will be reborn with that knowledge that we as a group are one. It can not be in the near future for if it were the man of science would be drawn in to examine and test those of us that return. It will be when the man of science has opened his ears and eyes, not to the fact that he can see and understand, but begin to listen to that which, as yet, he is not prepared to do. The time will come when groups such as this group with which I am, will come into the world in many groups and the mind of man will expand and understand, knowing that he too is part of another group aiming for all groups to become one in survival and wisdom, and dwelling within the mind of the human form."

"Do you understand?"

The group thanked Soren again for a most interesting evening and agreed they were already looking forward to their next meeting.

6

COMMUNICATION BETWEEN WORLDS

"You speak of the infiltration of Wisdom and yet all wisdom lies in the heart of man – being within the mind of man; it is simply that man has become deafened and overcome by the activities of the world and his own desires. How is it done? It is done with difficulty and yet in itself it is simple. If the minds of men were as open as they are claimed to be, then the connections could be made directly into each and every individual of your world. But in the world of Spirit the vibrations that surround us are of varying degrees, as they are around you. I refer to that which we spoke of last week – as above, so below. In the world of Spirit it happens that those on the lower levels of the astral planes will draw very close to the man of Earth, and man is often deceived by these lower entities. In so saying, we are *not* saying that these low entities are evil beings, but they are on the whole, in the majority attracted to the vibrations of the world and its people, so therefore you, as physical beings with minds that are becoming awakened by the knowledge that there is something more than this life, should be reaching and stretching forth that mind-capacity to join in union with those of higher levels.

In your world, those that work on various levels are often referred to by your mediums as being those of higher levels, and they in truth know nothing. Sometimes we of Spirit become frustrated with those who are more concerned with what we were, rather than what we are. I refer to your inquiry earlier brother, whereby you wished to know more about Soren, but Soren is not *one*. Soren belongs to, and is part of a group of Souls that have walked together since the beginning without knowledge, as so do you as singular individuals, and are governed and overlooked by those in Spirit with whom you belong as a group, and your individual single lives, on your attainment to a degree of Spiritual knowledge and wisdom, will return to you in full. You are taught that you, as an individual on this Earth, will only remember this, but in truth you do not know if your individuality is as limited as you at present believe it is. It may well be, and with some of you, that when you return to the Spirit world, you will remember many lives. But as a Group Soul you will not only remember *your* lives, but the lives of your group as individual human beings, for you will have access to their experiences on the Earth plane. It is not just the Earth in which any one of you or any one of us have lived, but we have lived in these various worlds with the knowledge hidden in the mind of man, but *open* to the mind of Spirit by which each one of us has experienced other Earth lives.

As to how does the wisdom infiltrate itself to you, it is done through degrees of vibration and ability of those in the lower levels. They are most important to those of us on a higher level, which enables us to communicate *indirectly,* but *directly* to you. You, as workers for Spirit, often describe yourselves as a telephone exchange, and in the time of your new way of life and communication, such knowledge will have a broader aspect in which to be delivered. We at the higher levels will use those lower levels of the astral plane to bring wisdom and knowledge of the life of Spirit to the Earth people.

Within your own group, within your own circle, are other circles and each circle observes the other in the limitation of their minds. Also in the limitation of the minds, you have observed, have had contact with, those which you would term a higher level. These occurrences are during your sleep state – they are during your times of mind emptiness, which unfortunately, in the world of man is very limited. We on the other hand are able to infiltrate information into the mind of man in full understanding that we have completed that work regardless of whether or not you, in the conscious state you find yourselves in now, are aware.

It may be that you will read many books and to read is of benefit to enable you to understand the various ways in which you as human beings can communicate in a Spiritual manner one to the other, and in so doing recognising another's superiority or limitations, and so it is in the world of Spirit. If we should say to you the level at which we are, would it be that you would be more interested in the fact that we came from a high level, than you would if we came from a lower? There are those from your world that have been waited for by many groups, because among you is the older Soul treading the physical plane and then on returning is the wisest of the group who waits. Therefore information can be given to you by a living being as well as those who are without physical form. It is a communication of minds, and wisdom is passed from one to another in silent form - without words - but with a full understanding of a complete lesson, and this is how we from a higher level transmit our words to those on a lower plane who are more capable in connecting their vibrations to yours. So as we teach, they learn, and as they teach you, you learn and so too in the levels above us. Man's mind is limited through his own restriction and not the limitation of that we call God, and we try to manifest and express from our own being and mental ability. We can only be what we can assume God to be and even those in higher levels do not, as yet, *truly know* this God!

When man leaves his Earth he is accepted and drawn into the group of which he has always been, but it can be eons of time before one will return. It does not mean that the incomplete group is not able to communicate *without* his help as all groups, whether it is one or two or many, are able to transmit their knowledge and their wisdom into the lower planes. As to *how* it is done: if you were to communicate with another you would use a telephone, or your computers. When we communicate with another in the Spirit world we communicate on a fine web of thought energy transference, and we can identify and acknowledge through a mental transmission the one with whom we wish to communicate, and this is how it is done on all levels of the astral plane. Now, if you speak of the planes that are above those, these guides communicate in a similar fashion, but on a finer vibration and their vibrations, as they reach into the lower realms of the astral field, are of Spirit – sometimes distorted – and it takes a number of specialist groups to work, to discover, to bring in to action, the form of transmission used. For do not forget, although we speak of the higher levels of Spirit, they are also different worlds and as you sit for communication so too do the groups sit in the astral planes and those above so we may communicate one to another.

I must say at this point that man is greedy for such information when he is unable to use that vibration which is within him; that he as an individual *could* communicate directly to the Godhead. But if he should, at this stage of progression, as a beginner, he would become mentally exhausted and in some cases totally deranged and others observing him would indeed commit him to an institution. But if man in his silence and stillness listened

to the voice that speaks words of wisdom and comfort, he would
be guided.

Many in our level are able to communicate freely with the
man of Earth, but it is for the man of Earth to judge that
communication. If it does not bring him comfort then he is *not*
reaching to higher levels. Man can only reach to a level of
communication and understanding that his present intelligence is
able to absorb, beyond that it would not be comprehensible, he
would simply not understand!

As the vibrations are lifted there is a sound which man has
described as a whining, a high pitched sound and he in his turn
then *assumes* he has reached a certain level of the Spirit world, but
he does not realise that the least sound, the nothingness, of
vibration shows the degree of his ability to reach those higher
levels, but man of Earth, because he hears with his physical ears,
assumes he has reached a *higher* level and will quote from those
levels. If you wish to learn true communication, then it must be in
silent dedication; we do not mean the silence of the world, but the
silence of man's mind. We cannot stress the importance of the
discipline of stillness, not just sitting still and disciplining
yourselves to a certain hour of the day. This is not as important as
some of your teachers will insist it is, the time of day does not
matter to the world of Spirit; because you have no understanding
of the time in Spirit you assume that your meditations must be at
certain times. It is immaterial. As you make a connection on a
higher realm it is automatically transmitted to your group. Each
Soul identifies with his own group; so therefore, if you are aiming
for true wisdom and communication from Spirit, learn to identify
the vibrations which are around you and in so doing you will
contact *your* group!

This may not seem to happen in your lifetime, but it may
have *already* happened in a previous life, for you are one with
your Soul group. It may be that you have walked the Earth plane
before and you have simply forgotten your connection with that
group. When you were a child you had to learn to walk and talk –
in a previous life you had to learn to walk and talk – and as you
have forgotten the physical ways of man then it must be you have
forgotten also the way of Spirit communication. If we were to
teach you in the way we would choose, it would be a natural
response from your Soul entity that if you allowed it to manifest
that ability to the conscious mind, man himself would be able to,

in that conscious state, connect with his own group. The familiarity that you would experience on seeing with your inner Soul-Self and hearing with that same Soul-Self would be as though in physical form and you had met once again a long-lost brother. Recognition would be instant! There would be no need for names and identification, or mode of dress, or identity in physical form – all would be in Soul identification. You yourselves, as brothers and sisters of an earthly plane, would not meet your Soul group in the gender in which you are at present; you would be welcomed as the Soul identity of the physical body! The physical body would be of no interest - although once communication had been made and experienced in its true form of Soul recognition of its group, the identification of the physical body would remain intact - until your return.

You are going through what one may term a trial of true identity. Once this is recognised within you, the transformation that you would physically experience would be the transformation of Soul identity, and although you would appear to be male or female, *that* identity would fall away from your minds and you would be Soul expression still in the form of male and female but without the flippancies attached to your gender. They would be of no importance, only in the identification of love between man and woman and the production of children.

When we speak of children of your Earth and the union of man and woman in Soul recognition, it is the union of the Souls that make manifest the physical child. The child in physical form is a manifestation in which a new Soul may reside. But it is the union of Souls which brings forth the new Soul into a physical body which is able to relate at a very young age to its naturalness of Soul and becomes aware of its Christ Self at an early age. Once this is attained, that Christ which has recognised itself as a newly formed Soul in a physical body, will be the child that leads the man!

We of Spirit are endeavouring through the vibrations of the different levels in the astral planes from a level *above* those planes, to make efficient connections. Do not become over-excited by the fact that we have stated that we are from above the astral planes, for we are still children seeking to teach and guide younger ones. We as yet have not reached our ultimate – that ultimate being the source of God – the return to the Godhead! But it is among your children on Earth who are now seeking beyond the realms of the astral planes, and it is because your own vibrational fields are becoming finer and you in physical form and understanding of total acceptance of your Soul-Selves are able to raise your own vibrations. If this should happen quickly in the world of man, we have already said what the outcome could be, but in so saying, there are some in the world that have reached the stage of finer vibrations and mental recognition of the Soul-Self and the physical mind being one, but once this has been accepted, then so too will the vibrations in man's mind and the world of men be raised.

It is beginning! Man is taking more notice of his surroundings and the living physical forms around him and the time is coming when man, in raising his vibration, will see the Soul entities of the living beings around him and in the world in which he lives. Man must learn to control his inquisitiveness until he has mastered himself. Once he has mastered his conscious mind he will then be able to enter into that which he terms the unconscious mind so he may link in complete harmony to the Greater Conscious Mind, whatever you wish to call that area in which all wisdom and knowledge is. We can only present to you in very small measure in the language of words. Once you have become aware of your True-Self and allowed this True-Self to *Become*, then the greater mind will be opened to you and you will *KNOW ALL THINGS!* At present it would not be wise, for man is as the child learning to walk – he needs to be aided and guided – as you would guide your own children, we guide you in the various levels of the astral planes and above.

It is hoped that you have understood the way in which we have tried to explain. Once you have this opening to your deeper wiser Soul-Self that is within, then this teaching will become as a child's realisation of what he can do with the alphabet; and once you have reached this realisation you will understand the vibrations between different levels of the astral planes and your questions can be directed to those in the higher levels and you will receive your answers from them."

Soren then said, "I hope you have an understanding of this talk and now perhaps I can answer one question you might wish to ask."

"Thank you, Soren, would you explain how you would incarnate next time on Earth and would you retain your existing wisdom and knowledge?"

Soren then answered with the following information:

"As I said earlier the newly born child must learn to walk and talk and I said that as man grows spiritually and at one with his Soul-Self then the ability to communicate with higher planes would be, and this also is part of that which would be retained in the mind of the child. And as it grows it would become familiar with its Soul-Self at an early age and the wisdom that dwells there which would manifest itself into that child's conscious mind. The child would come to adulthood in a spiritual sense, at a very tender age possibly as young as twelve to fifteen of your years.

In the time of *our* return that exception will be accepted by a great number of your people and these young ones would be referred to as prodigies. They would be termed as 'highly intelligent beings' but at that particular time the majority of the world of men will also be in communication with their Higher-Selves. We, who return at that point, will return with still extra knowledge of communication between the minds of our group and we would be the teachers of the man on Earth. Yes, we *will* be born with that knowledge, with that wisdom, with that understanding, and in a short time this would be made manifest and acceptable, but at present this would not be."

"Does that answer your question?"

The group thanked Soren once again for the enlightening evening and agreed it was time to close until next time.

7

DIRECTION ON NEGATIVITY

Soren's remarks this particular evening were directed to one of our members who had been very upset by the negative reaction of her mind towards another's cruel action, and concerned the effect this had on her spiritual progression.

Another question related to Nostradamus and his prognostications in relation to time.

"It is difficult for man on Earth to not suffer the pain of bitterness, for it is in the trials of your world from the beginning of the time of your world when man first stood upright and looked beyond himself and that with which he could identify, to understand that there was something much further, much more powerful, much greater than he himself, and although this knowledge was limited in his mind he *did* recognise the grandeur of the spaces around him and in these spaces created that which we call God.

The world in itself has been fraught with bitterness, and bitterness casts a shadow upon and around your world. It fills the Auric Fields of man, and that in itself emanates one to another and it emanates also in to the world of Spirit. We who offer to come forward to teach are sometimes often reluctant to walk into that vale of darkness, for we too, can become absorbed by bitterness, but we understand bitterness to be a human failing and not a natural element of the Soul, in which lies the power to lift one above that energy – for in itself it is an energy. It is a destructive force that pulls man down to the depths of despair. It is only through recognising the pain that bitterness inflicts upon the heart of man and creates a fogging of his mind, that he realises this pain is not good, but in itself necessary, for it brings to mind with shock of the horror of the thought that he has entertained, as with our sister this evening who felt great bitterness over the act of an unkind neighbour and her reaction to that act. It is by recognising this state of mind, which in itself is pulling man's energies down, that he realises that it is through the uplifting of the physical heart and mind which then joins in relationship with the Soul that is within the physical body of man. If you understood that aspects of pain, in whatever guise it should come to you, is the part of the lesson of man to associate Self with Soul, and in so doing becomes strengthened by the presence of Soul.

You question what is the aim of God that you should suffer to walk this plane without knowing in which direction you are heading, and the answer is that you are in the direction you are meant to be! You are at the crossroads of life at the time you were meant to be. It is a time of spiritual growth, yet man will say, "How, when I am pulled to the depths of despair and suffer the pain of bitterness, how is it part of my growing process? How is it that I am classed by Spirit as an evolving human Soul?" We say it is because as these occurrences pass in your lives you will overcome them! There will be losses, there will be pain, there will be recognition of your own weakness, but in these recognitions will also be the power of the Soul that guides you.

The Soul in itself does not participate in the steps which the human takes. He does not guide the man on his physical path, he guides the man in his emotional and mental state, and guides it to a place of strength; and it is only in this place of strength – in this time of silence – that the Soul can draw into the energy field of man to invigorate and strengthen that one. All be it, you will still undergo the pains of your world, but the fact that you overcome and awaken the following day with a new energy - although it may seem that energy is not as responsive as your negative action - it *is* the energy that helps you to partake of the steps that are necessary to remove yourselves from those conditions. It *is* that there will be losses and these losses are not regained, but the lesson learned by them is of value to man's mind. There are times in the pathway of man when you must fight fire with fire! You may consider this to be a negative action or a negative reaction to a situation in which you find yourselves, but this is also a world of survival – not survival of the fittest in the sense that you have been taught by other teachers of your world – but the fittest in the ability to communicate with the Soul energy that promotes you and walks with you in your path of material gains and losses. When man passes into the spiritual world he is also faced with the negativities of his own actions. Now this, at Soul level, in another form of body *similar* to the one in which you at present reside, consists of greater mental control of his physical *in that form* and emotion and mental senses (for there is always another body that takes the place of the previous body). The Soul in its walking in the spiritual world will again be faced with the bitterness of another's action against him. The Soul is guided by the Spirit entity of the God-breath – life force – God- strength – with which he will overcome these negativities. This is experienced in the first level of the astral plane, that level you call the Summerland. That Summerland experience can help to overcome these negativities if you so wish to use the powers which are within you, both in the material world and the world of Spirit – these are the powers of forgiveness and acceptance - forgiveness toward the other and acceptance of your own situation. Your reply to that could be that the situation has caused *you* great financial loss or great mental and emotional pain, but you are reaching for the power of your Soul-Spirit body to enter into the physical form and the thinking mind of man, in the sense of Spirit union. Once this has been attained all that you will face will be *small mountains* – it is your *way* of acceptance that creates things to become larger than they truly are! When man steps upon this Earth he comes with all the power and strength of the Soul that enters with him, but sometimes the Soul in itself, although supplying strength and power, neglects to bring into the mind of man the importance of loving his enemy. Let us understand what is meant by the enemy of man. It is not your neighbour, it is not others who rule your world, your greatest enemy is Self - the part of you that weakens and becomes bitter under strain! As you progress you will recognise these negativities within you, and as you do you will draw in the breath of Spirit, the access of immediacy with God, to overcome these negativities that are *yours*. In overcoming, no matter what the loss may be, you will be at one with Self, you will be content, and you will be filled with joy that you have allowed the Soul entity to lift you, the human, to a level of mental progression. The Soul in itself is becoming the victor of the earthly path. The cost, you may feel is at your expense – the mental way of man of thinking and acting – but as you in physical form become more familiar with your Soul-Self desire and the Spirit nature and the God-Self of which you are, then with mental, emotional physical form you will experience the joy of God.

You, as individuals, are at different levels of spiritual growth to your brothers and your sisters and this is *why* you are filled with bitterness and anger at different times, and are yet still shocked by your reaction because your Soul has brought forward that recognition, so therefore be glad, be joyful that you as individuals, have evolved to that degree. As we have said before, the Soul that is within does not evolve, it *progresses* on its journey to experience the earthly way of life and the only way it can is through physical form and with man's emotions, with his desires and his *free will*. If on facing a pain, an upheaval, something that is saddening to you, and you can face it with the strength of your Soul, you as a man, a thinking being with free will, would accept the way of the Soul and your free will would be in union with your own Soul's mental growth.

It is a long journey and yet it does not consist of one lifetime, it consists of one complete whole in various schools of physical advancement and it is known by those of us in Spirit that the majority of you who are seeking the light of God will grow in honour of your Soul-Self. Your wisdom and your knowledge will have accumulated over many lifetimes, and it may seem at this particular point in your lives you are burdened with the cares of your world and you ask, "What is it that God wants? – what is it they want and what is it my Soul wants?" You consist of Soul, of Spirit, of God and if you separate your selves, you know in your mental alertness the Soul, the Spirit, the God, wants only good, so therefore that which you are endeavouring to achieve on your Earth plane must only be for the good of your physical selves! You cannot take upon yourselves the burdens of others' crosses, your own crosses at these early stages of development are heavy enough, but you can put your crosses upon the God-Spirit. We do not mean you lay your problems at the Feet of God and ask him, for God dwells within you and this means that you are laying your burdens at your *own* feet! You are responsible beings, the Soul that dwells within you has chosen that particular path you walk, thereby call upon – be still with – and be at ease with your Soul being and your answers will come in the form of natural gentle stillness of your mind. In the stillness of your mind you will learn true acceptance, you will learn Soul acceptance, and in so learning these qualities you will be able to apply them to Self, and as you face the obstacles in your world, that Soul-Self which you have allowed, will help you overcome and your outcome will be that of joy. It cannot be any other way, for you have consciously given your destiny to the Soul-Spirit-God that is within you. You are *allowing* the power of God to guide you, for that power is your power - it is your Soul power, your Spirit power.

In your world are many beings who are not as strongly connected spiritually with Soul-Self, and these are the ones at this particular point you are addressing; and in addressing them you are recognising that you, as physical beings, will not allow yourselves to become as they are. As was said earlier by our sister, she was horrified at the thoughts that she had, but they were natural thoughts and in recognising this they immediately attained for her a boost, a lift, in recognising her failure and eliminating it. That thought will not enter her mind again, she will have gained by it, and it is the finished action of mind and will not occur again.

If, when man in his true realisation of his true self being that Soul, becomes *one* with Soul and allows the Buddhic nature within to manifest, then that becomes truly acceptable, he can then look upon the mountain and know that in one step he can overcome that mountain, and the mountain immediately falls away – it becomes a shadow on the wall. It is illuminated by the light of knowledge and anything illuminated by the light of knowledge gains Wisdom. For the light brings forth that which is of very little value in the sense of the world, but the light of spiritual knowledge and spiritual understanding allows the physical man to emanate his true Soul-Self and in your struggle you are beginning to realise this is so. Vaguely – dreamily at first – but it is there, the awakening of your true potential!

There will be more successes in your lives than failures. As you overcome a failure and look back on it you will recognise it as a learning process. When you look back at your victories you will recognise them as being a victory of Soul-man. You will have evolved from your animalistic nature to your Soul nature. This is approaching fast in your world and there are many such as you who are meeting great obstacles and yet persevere and overcome them. It is the time of the Soul-awakening of the world, and this process will be – must be – for man is awakening to True Self, True Spirit, True God within!

The path is strewn with many little pebbles and stones and is painful to the physical heart and mind of man, but eventually, in your lifetimes, these stones and jagged pebbles will become smooth boulders on which you will be able to stand and overlook your kingdoms, your successes, knowing that as an individual man and woman you have walked this earthly plane hand in hand with

Soul-Self and the Soul is blending in gently to the physical body. You become two beings blending as ONE and the possibility then can be that you do not go to that Summerland other than for a very brief period. You will evolve; you will grow further into the world of Spirit in which you truly belong. You are indeed disciples on a path and surely the fact that you have been on this path for a number of years must show you, as early man, standing upright, that there is something greater and grander and more beautiful outside of yourselves, and as you look toward this beauty you will recognise that beauty is you in physical form emanating true Soul vibration!"

The group thanked Soren and his brothers for given such an explanatory talk and they were very impressed with him and his supporting group of brothers, to which Soren replied:
"May I just say with your reference to us being brothers? We are neither brothers nor sisters; we are neither male nor female. There is no physical gender. We are one union of Soul-Spirit-God".
Soren added that there would be time for one question.
The question as usual came from the inquisitive Mark.
"You have said that time is a man-made concept and in the spirit world you say that time does not exist and yet I am sure you are familiar with the philosopher, Nostradamus, who prognosticated certain things would happen. Could you explain in the simplest of forms, how this thinking happened and how these people can identify what is going to happen in the future, or what is time?"
Soren answered: "Time is non-existent. Time is something that in itself is *still* through which man passes, but those who have foretold the future of man in the years to come, and I must use your language, know of the time of these events in the way of *man's thinking*, but if you study the predictions of the ancients you will discover that very often all of these events, in a small or large measure, can happen in every decade, in every century, in every millennium. You associate, interpret and believe in what Nostradamus and many others have stated, and yet if you study the works of Nostradamus you will find vagueness and the elimination of time in itself.
    What he has foretold is the figures that are in and around at a particular time when these activities happen, but not of time

itself. It is often when man interprets any work of the ancient workers he must give a *time* and *date*, but what we of Spirit try to explain to you is that time consists of when the *event has reached its expression of that era.* Nostradamus and many others, and in reference to your holy books, speak of the end of time. Time has never existed. It is the end or the beginning of events, and a time given is when the events will happen. But it does not mean a particular year. It is difficult to explain the work of others. When man has learned to project his mind into a future happening, *time,* correctly, he can only eliminate the actions that are around at that moment specified. It is the result of the action that brings about a *time.* He may well have said - if he knew the word - it would be during the time of your nuclear bombs or your invention of television or of the telephone or of your computers, *then* you could estimate the time correctly. There have been many powers, events, many happenings within the world of man to which you could state that Nostradamus and many others intended these events to be. Do you understand?"

"Yes thank you, it brings a clearer understanding of the concept of 'time'. But Soren, before you go," continued Mark jokingly, "in time I will 'catch you up' and eventually 'floor you' with my questions!"

Amid laughter Soren went on to say: "It is so difficult, your word 'time'. For instance, your Christ, when he spoke to the people of your world over two thousand years ago - you can estimate the time of his birth, but you cannot prove it and this is how it is with predictions. Man can only estimate - estimation in the form of time can take eons of time or short time. Do not be too involved with time, time in Soul essence is as nothing, it is as breath taken. You breathe without noticing, therefore let time pass through you or you through it. It happens you are the mover – time in itself is non-existent!"

"Bless you, thank you for coming.*"*

8

WINGS OF PROTECTION

"I would speak tonight about that which you term the 'Wings of Protection' and in asking the Father God to create this protection around you, you yourselves have come to the conclusion that you are *unable* to protect yourselves. It is not that God or Spirit cannot intervene in your lives, but *you* have been given the power of Spirit, of Soul and the God-Self which will enable you to create that protective energy that is so badly needed to be expressed in the world of man. Man has become sensitive only to his desires and not the cruelties of the world, the cruelties you inflict one upon another. Man has become secretive in his way, in that he denies entry into his being by his fellow brothers and sisters. He does not give all that he truly is to another and *yet* man dedicates himself to the path of Spirit to walk in the footsteps of the Christ and the great prophets that have gone before, and they in their time were open to all the judgments and the influences, the cruelties and the love of the world in which they walked. So too it is with the man on Earth to this day, but the barrier of protection that man creates is filled with antagonism that dares another to enter or intervene in man's life. He is *not* using the power of protection – the God-given gift that lies within.

When man asks God for protection he assumes that God will build a barrier through which no one can enter. But this you know is a falsehood, because as man becomes influenced by Spirit and the physical beings around him, he can become affected by the energies that they are creating themselves and that interference occurs. Man is left physically and mentally exhausted by the attacks of others which may *not* intentionally be filled with malice. It may be that the one to whom these attacks have been directed has become weakened by the day's progress and as an unprotected being he is then submissive to the pains involved.

What *is* the protection you are asking? How do you envisage this protection to be? Do you expect a barrier of stone, a barrier of love, or a barrier to defend yourself from all the ailments of the world and if this is so, then understand this is not the way of

God! God has given you everything you *need* in this world to protect, to defend, to be victorious, to overcome, and to eliminate your own anxieties with the power of divine love that dwells within, so therefore it must be that you – as a follower – are able to construct that defence mechanism. 'What', you will ask, 'is it made of? How can I construct this form of protection around myself and those I love?' It may be that you will do this physically; it may be that you will lock the doors of your home to protect yourself and your family, but what if the intrusion comes from the world of Spirit? The protection you ask for – *as* you ask it – is already being constructed, if you are believers in the power that God has given to you! This may seem a little confusing, because many Souls are dependent upon their earthly teacher, believing that teacher can bring the protection needed and to those of us that gather around your circles and meetings, this is *partly* true, but in the same instance those on the lower levels of the astral plane can inflict their presence amongst you. So therefore, how is man to protect himself? Man has an inbred understanding of total survival – not of his physical self – but of the Soul-Self that is within the physical being, and this Soul-Self is able to create a protection that not only keeps the Soul safe but also that of the physical form!

This protection is created through very fast vibrations that create denseness because with that protective system is the denseness of earthly matter. The denseness, the slow vibration and the fast vibration combine, and in their combination create what you might term a 'sticky' substance – not as such to the touch of the hand – but to the vibration of what one can sense. Within that wall of protection the Soul is able to communicate freely with his physical being and those of others outside that wall of protection, so therefore, understand as you ask in earnest, in truth, in faith in yourself and the power of God, that wall of protection is raised.

Now what of those who are new to your understanding? They are dependent on those that are around them and this being the case, the Soul that is within that one, without that one's knowledge, is creating that boundary wall with the help of those other entities in that same circle of physical beings. If man is attacked by a lower entity the Soul immediately withdraws into itself, not to *escape* from its physical home, but to *protect* the physical home in closing its own Auric Field. The one that is being abused by the low entity will feel as if he is filled with faith in the god which he worships and will feel a tightening of the skin as though a very 'light plastic' has been placed around him – breakable, but also protective! For it is in the mind of man that the protection *is* - although it has been *created* by the Soul entity for the physical being - the Soul will protect that one from mental affliction.

There are some instances when that protective way is not sufficient, but this is usually because the physical being has weakened in his ability of communicating with Spirit or with the teacher of his group. In most cases the damage done *is* repairable, but sometimes in your world the one who has initially been damaged will succumb to further attacks. What then should man do, what should Spirit do? There is very little that man himself can do and indeed very little that Spirit can do! It then rests with the doctors of your world who will decide if these are psychological problems and very often these are diagnosed as schizophrenic – but this is not always the case! There are very few instances of true schizophrenia! More often than not, it is the result of an astral attack. It may seem strange for Spirit to speak of such things and can at this point put fear into the mind of man, for he then will believe that Spirit cannot – or will not – protect him as he enters into the place of knowing nothing, but this is not so. As man progresses in his belief in God, in Spirit, in Soul-Self and Self he becomes stronger. He consciously erects that wall of protection in union with his Soul-Self and any assault is immediately recognised and man will act accordingly, fully conscious of his actions and in full communication and co-operation with his Soul-Self.

It is the way of the Soul - within the physical body – and it has learned over eons of time to be aware of his communication with the physical being, all be it that the physical being's conscious mind is not always aware. It is only a period of time and more so in *this* generation of life on Earth, that this oneness has began. But in so speaking of this oneness between Soul and man, not all men are fully aware of that link solidifying in the form of protection. You may say if man is not aware of his Spirit communication created by the Soul entity, then of what value is it to the unconscious mind? It is in *preparation* for a further life that that Soul will undertake on the physical plane, during which he *will* become aware of his ability and his communication with Self to create that protection, but it is hoped that when man can consciously do this he will be filled with the wonder and ability of Spirit communication, then when he creates that wall of defence he will harm no-one and no-one will harm him and those he loves. He will learn to extend that protection around his loved ones.

You are already being taught to create a light of love around yourselves and those you love, and the colour that is usually chosen is gold. This is to bring your imagination to the act you have undertaken. In your imagination you are 'seeing' this gold light around yourselves and those you love, but in actual fact you are joining with your Soul-Selves to create that substance drawn from the etheric and the physical world, to create that wall of protection. It will be in future generations of conscious effort that man will learn to do this, as Spirit, and the Soul that has gone before you have learned, usually in the etheric world, but now the same ability is coming to the world of man to use.

If man were to use this now in a conscious manner, it would cause chaos and confusion, for others would see the result of this protective wall and yet not understand it and again there would be further investigation into *man* and not *Spirit,* nor *Soul,* and not the truth of God. Man being what he is – Soul, Spirit and God, would be 'dissected' as such, by your men of science and of the medical profession because they cannot and will not identity two beings, being in one, but in so saying this, the time will come when all people from the birth age into the old age will learn how to create this wall! It will not isolate the individual but will bring comfort to the seeking Soul of man. It will bring comfort to the inquiring mind in man and his furthering of spiritual knowledge will be uninterrupted by those who will sadly not accept the power of Spirit. But these numbers will eventually diminish, and as we have said so many times, God will walk this Earth.

When we say 'God will walk this Earth', are we saying then that this God will come to Earth with this wall of protection that he himself has created around himself? We are *not* saying this, for the God that walks the Earth will be the God clothed in the *body of man* but in *full manifestation!* GOD TO MAN IS STILL THE EMBRYO!!! The embryo that dwells *in* man, is seeking the light of spiritual *acknowledgment* and the *recognition* of all men and *when* this happens God in true glory will manifest to that great extent to the most powerful *Being* in the form of Man!

When this all happens man will have learned to truly love the stranger amidst him, because he will love him as a brother Spirit. He will not recognise him in the physical form as brother, but certainly in the spiritual sense and there will be a *union* of

Souls. As we spoke of when *we* return, this union of Souls in groups of men who have learned to use the power of the Soul that is within, and recognition will be instant!

As man progresses and becomes aware of his true relationship to the Soul, he will meet great adventures in other worlds. This will not delay man's progress, indeed it may hasten it, for man will draw together to protect his world and its people, and *again* it will be the beginning of that emanation of that protective veil which will not just cover man and his loved ones, but men and their world! It may be during that time your own return may happen, this you will discover as you enter the world of Spirit to reflect upon the life you have led and the life you may wish to lead in a further incarnation. It may be you will return as teachers or perhaps, again as the pupil, but in whatever way you return, you will return knowing how to protect yourself, your Soul entity and guard the Spirit of love within yourself and those you love."

"Do you understand?"

The group agreed that they understood and thanked Soren for speaking to them that evening.

Soren then addressed Mark, "And my inquisitive friend, who will one day 'floor me'. Do you have a question for me that I may answer?"

Soren had addressed this question to the young man because the previous week he had said he would eventually 'catch up' with Soren and 'floor' him. Soren reminded him of this and continued to say, "When you do, it will be time for you to become the teachers and this is what we in Spirit hope, so that when we *return, you* will be teachers with advanced spiritual knowledge and will help us to attain that knowledge which we will need at much younger ages. But for the moment ask your question."

"Soren, my question is: could you take me to the astral planes and bring me back whilst in physical form?"

"You are taken most nights!"

"I am taken most nights, am I?" Mark remarked surprised, as Soren continued.

"Man on the whole is taken most nights but he is not always consciously aware of this, for he is taken in his Soul-aware conscious state. He feels he has been in a dream land or he has been in a place of nothing and of no-one and of silence. In the varying degrees of sleep, the Soul part of you escapes and returns to that with which he is familiar. It may be with the extension of Soul-mind that the Soul will return to the past or to the future of man himself. It may be he will return to the schools of learning, it may be that he goes to the universities in the world of Spirit or it may be that the Soul is on a journey of rescue work. Have there not been times in your lives when you have woken and been totally exhausted? This is sometimes when the Soul returns from 'rescue work' and its exhaustion is transmitted to the physical body!

This happens – but your question is really why are you not totally consciously aware of being in the world of Spirit? It may be, and this is not meant rudely, that your Soul may be encumbered by you. It may be that your Soul willingly takes you, but in the time between sleep and release, man's mind – as active as it is – is unable to totally trust and go with his Soul-Self. The Soul recognising and acknowledging this will return on its own to the world of Spirit. But there are amongst you those that have entered these mysteries and joys of the Spirit world and have come back with complete recollection of where they have been and with whom they have been and of what they have learned and of what they have seen.

It is often that man will relate times of trauma in your world that are so detailed in their conscious mind, that they truly feel they were there – in truth they were. Very often the Soul that dwells within is in an advanced state, enabling it to offer wisdom to the mind of man, but the mind may not as yet be mature enough to absorb the information, but it may be that during that man's life the information given to him will come to the surface. It *could* be this life!

If you ask could I take you to the astral plane, it is for your teacher or guide to take you and if I took you, would you indeed *know* me? It could be one of my group, but more likely it would be one of your own group, for you belong to a group, as do the others present this evening.

If you wish to enter the world of the astral planes, when you pray or request to be taken to the schools of knowledge, to the universities, to the place where the children live and learn happily the way of Spirit and if you wish to meet those you have loved in this life, ask also that! Your request *will* be granted in time, it is for you to retain the memory. When you say farewell to your Soul-Self on its preparation to leave and then later on its return, say to yourself "I will remember where I have been taken", and if you can sleep with that thought firmly in your mind, your Soul-Self will impress upon your mind all its experiences, and you will retain it. It takes time, practice and dedication. It does not always happen, but there will be. times when you will return with *full* recollection of your experiences in the world of Spirit. In so saying of your guide it does not mean that I may not 'pop along'!"

Amid laughter the questions continued.

"Would you be able to manifest yourself to us at present, Soren?"

"No!" Soren replied.

"You would not be able?"

"I would not do it!"

"You would not do it?"

"I did not say I would not be *able* to, I said I would *not* do it! This one *(referring to the channel)* is not prepared in the physical and mental state she needs to be for that form of manifestation. It is an entirely different way of work for Spirit and the channel. It involves great energies on both sides. This one has not been prepared for that kind of mediumship and it is not expected from the world of Spirit that she should do so. It is time now for me to go and I have enjoyed this evening and it seems we are more relaxed! Thank you and God bless you."

"Thank you, Soren. I still intend to 'catch you up'!"

Soren replied quietly, "We'll see!"

9

REBIRTH, LOVE, TRANSITION AND DEATH

"I would speak to you of rebirth, I would speak to you of love, I would speak to you of transition and I would speak to you of death; and when we look upon these four aspects we are speaking of life and when we speak of life, we are speaking of the progression of Soul in the evolution of the physical body of man. And what is love that we should make such greatness of it? Love is that which sustains all things – love is that which one declares to another. Love is that which enables man to protect himself and those that he is in care of.

When we speak of love we use it as a term of gentle endearment. We use it as a term of loyalty to our countries. We use it as a term loosely, and it is abused - for in truth, man does not understand love. When we speak of life it covers all aspects of those words which I just spoken. When we speak of transition it is the journey from birth to death. It is the journey from death to life and this is how life is. Life is constant. Life is that which you call God and it is from that aspect of God, from that source of divinity, that all things evolve - and yet man in his sorrow complains bitterly of the way in which love has dealt with his life. He complains bitterly of the time it takes to take one step to another so that he may find comfort and richness of heart and at the end of his physical life he weeps and wails the fact that he has not had the successes which he feels are his due right – and who is to blame, but man himself! For God has given to man all the necessities he needs to make this transition through life successful. Man, in his understanding, in the spiritual sense, of the way of transition, assumes it to be only a term used as he evolves from the ignorant being into the Soul-aware man and this is so. There are others who believe the transition is from the time of birth, whereby man learns to become intelligent and to use that intelligence to become rich in his life and to leave his riches to those he loves and die in peace and so too, is this true. But transition in its true sense is the co-operation between the physical heart and mind to the total acknowledgment and awareness of his Soul-Self!   This is the greatest transition man takes in his life!

It is not for man to become successful in the eyes of others but it is for man to become successful in his own way of thinking and in his own eyes, whereby he may stand tall knowing he has completed that transitional period. But you may ask 'What experiences must I undergo to reach my goal of Soul awareness?' The lesson man must learn is to be still and at peace with himself. He must learn to accept himself exactly as he is and not to try to improve, nor to lessen, nor to give away all he has accumulated in life, it is simply being a man who becomes truly aware of his Soul-Self. For it is only in its stillness, man's mind and heart during his transition period, that he becomes familiar with the Soul's needs. In becoming familiar with this he will recognise in his own stillness that the needs of his *Soul* are also *his* needs! This could be termed as relinquishing his free-will, but this is not so. Man does not relinquish his free-will to God in a submissive manner - he gives it freely and gladly knowing in his mental capacity that which he gives up, that which he sacrifices is as nothing. For the true path of the Soul is to enlighten man's mind to this knowledge and when it is fully acceptable, all that man in his thinking mind wants falls away and his desire is to complete the transition between his mental, his physical, his emotional being to the submission to that of his spiritual growth. We are not speaking of the Soul, we are speaking of man's spiritual growth – *this* is the transition period!

When we speak of death we do not speak of the death of the physical body, but the death of the duration that it has taken *for* this transitional period to pass, and it can be on man's deathbed itself, it can be on his rebirth into another life, or it can be into the full of the life he is living now. If it is to become in the full of the life he is living now it is a time of great joy, of great happiness, of great love of the Self, for in loving the Self the Soul has a completely free and open outlet for its expression and in Soul expression comes true spiritual awareness of the needs of man and his brothers, and in true spiritual awareness comes the God-flow and man loves his brother in the true sense of the word. On man's deathbed it *should* be that man is joyous at this occasion, for there will be no fear of physical pain of the dying body, there will only be an awareness of freedom of the mind and the emotion enclosing itself into the Soul body of man through which it leaves the physical body.

Man is reluctant to leave the physical body, for it has become most precious to him, and yet the physical body is slowly decaying throughout its life on this Earth and the time you have to spend upon this world is a time that should be used in full understanding that it is the Soul's progression in gathering the harvests of life – your lessons – your experiences – your joys and your tears – into that Soul mind capacity, whereby it is strengthened and it enables the Soul to go further on the pathways of life, thereby coming to rebirth.

It is often asked by man, 'When one rebirths, how is it that he cannot remember all that he has experienced in a previous life'. If it were to be that man has total recall of that which he has done in previous lives it would cause confusion to the infant mind, whereby in itself it would have reached physical adulthood, physical mentality, but without physical growth; and there would be confusion in that young mind for in itself it would be fully adult, but in the eyes of others it would be a child and if that which you have done in a previous life was not pleasing to the young – the young life with the adult mind – this could cause mental confusion in that young body and all his previous experiences would be of no value. For it is not the experiences in themselves that are of value to the Soul, but the *reaction* to the experiences, whether they be of joy or sorrow. It is this which impinges itself upon the Soul mind, the young reborn being of that Soul has an understanding of values of life without being taught these lessons, and he will know instinctively right from wrong! Now, in saying this you will reply that the young child has to be taught the ways of right and wrong, but if you are familiar with the ways of the very young you will note in their eyes and in their reactions, that they are wiser in their spiritual understanding than they are in their mental understanding, and within that spiritual mind is a *knowing*. We spoke of the time in which we, as a group and other groups, will return, and the young ones that are around you now are the *beginning* of the returning Souls. When we speak of the returning Souls it does not mean that these Souls have not been on your Earth before, it simply means that this is the period in the Soul progression for these Souls to return with a *knowing* remembered in the physically formed mind. It will be during your lifetimes, perhaps towards the end, when you will notice a coming together of young minds who are far more advanced than you have been in your lifetimes but in a way of inner understanding, inner knowledge, and they will be the ones who will open the door wider than yourselves have been able, but it is for you as established human beings with Soul awareness to help these young ones! Again when we speak of death and rebirth these occurrences are constantly with you every hour of your day. There are new thoughts that enter your minds which create a rebirth. There is a thought that leaves your minds which created negativity within yourselves and those around you and it will leave your mind and this is *death!* It is not in the physical sense of death, but it is in the initial spiritual growth of your minds."

At this point Soren referred to a member of the group who had shown concern over a property he was interested in buying.

"You brother, are concerned about a property that you will purchase and we would tell you that when you see it, you will know it to be the one; but it is for you to discipline your eyes and your ears and your mind until that property arises – for it will – and it will be so clear in your mind's eye and your way of establishing and obtaining this property, that when it happens it will be as though a glove has been fitted over your hand. You will know and understand that this is your venue and this time the situation and circumstances around you will be correctly placed, endeavouring you to have that freedom you need. All will be well with you but it is for you to discipline that flittering mind that darts in all directions. Give your Soul time and the opportunity to bring your conscious mind to the place and time of your property."

Soren then resumed his lesson.

"When we speak to one another of a Soul desire, what man must understand is that Soul desire must not be placed for a selfish reason. Very often others will say it is so and often man himself will believe he *is* being selfish, but as we have told you in your times of circle development, you are here for your own progression and that is how it is for those who wish to develop spiritually within their own ability, within their own surroundings, within their own wants and desires; and when you begin to understand that that which you reach for yourselves is not for self-gratification, then will come the death of the old ways and the rebirth of the new. Man is in a state of transition – your world is in a state of transition. This is the beginning of Soul awareness throughout your world. When we say rebirth, it is because Soul awareness has been on your Earth many times, but man in his greed has made the opportunity become less and less among the common man. He must stand tall and be reborn into the knowledge and understanding of his own spiritual Self and walk his path. When man truly understands and acts upon the spiritual wisdom that is entering his physical mind then he will come upon another period of transition, but that road in which all activity will be, will become more uplifting for him for he will be strengthened by his decision. So, in your re-birth, in your time of transition and at your time of death, it is the time *throughout*, of love and life; for if man cannot love himself then he cannot possibly love life and if he cannot love life then he has no experience of love. This man can deny, for you all have a love of something in your lives, but the greatest thing you can love at this time of your lives is not your partners or your children, but your Self and by Self we mean the little Soul that resides within filled with the Spirit of Breath. For is this not God? As you love Self you love God, and if you love God you love that which is good, and if you love good you love life and you love the time of transition. You will look forward to your times of rebirth on a daily basis, and your times of death, for death is a passing of a lesson, it is *not* the ending of life, for life is everlasting.

When we speak of life we are speaking of everything entailed in that act of living, and in that act it entails the use of those periods of birth, transition and death. It is a time of great excitement, it is a time of great activity and by activity we do not mean in a physical sense, although this can be involved, it is a time of mental understanding of the Soul-Self; and in that understanding then the Soul-Self can express its Self in a mental clarity which it desires. It desires to live, it desires the time of transition, it desires its rebirth and its death, and in these things happening with the co-operation of the conscious mind of man, all aspects of life are overcome and the Soul will love that man of which he is part. Man and Soul become one on the 'Wheel of Life'."

"Do you understand?"

The group thanked Soren for his teaching and replied they did understand.

Soren continued: "I have no doubt in my mind or the mind of my group as to who will ask the question tonight!"

The group laughed and Mark ventured, "I wonder who that will be?" to which Soren replied, "Yes, I wonder?"

Mark continued, "Soren, you talk about worlds and I accept we live in a multidimensional world, but my question is, are there physical worlds like ours in the universe?" to which Soren replied:

"This question has been asked before by many of your people. No two worlds are totally alike but there are great similarities, but what man must understand is that there are worlds that are closer or further away from their suns, and there are worlds that may have two suns, also there are worlds that are larger or smaller and the physical forms of these beings will differ slightly. The slightness of difference may not be pleasing to those of different worlds, but they will be acceptable over a short period of time, but what is important, the beings on the other worlds are governed by Souls, such as your own Soul Self. There is no identity as such to the Soul for it is an aspect of that Great Divine. When we speak of different worlds, there are worlds much further away than the galaxies of which you are aware, and indeed the worlds of which you have very little knowledge have also life upon them of which your people have no understanding. Not *all* beings live on the *outside* surfaces, as does the man of Earth. Some are enclosed within the shell of that planet. That planet or world may appear to man to be barren, but *all* worlds are hives of activity in some form or another. Man is fearful that the beings of other worlds may be aggressive on meeting, but can that also not apply to the man of Earth? Do you not, if you are in fear of the unknown, gather the ones that you love to yourselves to protect and is this not what the beings of another world would do against you? It is for your world and other worlds to become Soul Aware, God Aware in the conscious understanding, so that when you come together, for you *will* come together, you will meet in harmony and well-being of Soul survival in physical form.

Your stargazers are looking with eyes that see only that which is physical. *If* they could improve and encourage the workings of mind communication, this is when worlds would come together in that *way* of communication, but this is something of the far distant future, although in limited form this way of communication has been achieved, not only by people such as yourselves, but by those of the scientific world! They are more advanced than they allow the common man to know, but not advanced enough to use that power in a sensible and sensitive way through which they could eliminate the sense of fear. If man could truly and honestly read his own and his brother's mind then there would be nothing to fear, for the need of good for oneself would be in all minds and this would be recognised by the stranger among you. But yes, these other worlds have life upon them in various stages of physical evolution, some more advanced and some less, but there is life!"

"Do you understand?"

"Yes, thank you, Soren and may I pose another question regarding the lesson last week?" The question came from Mark. "You mentioned in advance that you would 'pop along' and you threw another thing to me. You said, how would I recognise you, and indeed, how would I recognise you?"

"It has taken a *week* for you to think of that?" Joked Soren, "I did not say I *would* 'pop along' I said I *might!* "

Mark continued, "But I have a precognition of how I would see you, but it obviously a million miles away as to how you would appear."

Soren answered, "If you have a precognition of how you would see me....then *that* is how I would appear to you, but so too could energies of a less friendly disposition. You would recognise me through the influence of the one I work with. There would be a sense of *knowing* through the one through whom I speak that I was Soren. There would be that pupil-teacher relationship between you and she – that is how you would know me. There would be a slight imprint of this one around me, she would be in my vibrational field, not as you see and know her but as you would sense her. This would have to be this way because you are unfamiliar with direct contact with Spirit, so therefore your vibrational field would not be finely tuned enough for you to recognise me as Soren, but as this channel, yes, for you would be using a different form of vibration field around you. It is simply because you are not in tune with the vibration of Spirit. But again, if you were to be taken *out of* body to meet those in the world of Spirit, you would be taken by one who was accustomed to your vibrational field and you would feel at ease."

"Do you understand?"

"Yes, thank you Soren, I understand."

Soren then continued:

"If you feel at one and comfortable with the vibrations around you, then you could enter into the astral planes with the one who would accompany you. You may not *see* him or her but you would be aware of the feeling of brotherhood, of comfort and safety. When I said last week I may 'pop along' it was noted that you were unsettled and disconcerted on the particular evening you attempted to astral project, and I would say that we and others of your world are not allowed to impinge ourselves into the privacy of your growth. We can only encourage and teach, we cannot persuade you against your will to act in a way that would not be in accord to your way and your desire. If you wish to enter the astral plane you must do so with a sense of comfort within yourself. If you are disturbed or reluctant your journey then would not be pleasant. The reason you were not successful is because *you* were not ready, and until you are it would not be advisable to try to force the issue. You must prepare yourself to enter the astral worlds safely. You will be ready when your Soul has been given access to your very busy mind. You must learn stillness and *then* with control over your physical and emotional conditions your journey into the astral world will be successful. But it takes practice and dedication."

"Do you understand?"

"Soren, another question please: When you visit us here do you actually see us or is it simply done through sound?" persisted the eager Mark.

"It is done on the sense of vibration, we 'see' and 'hear' you but as a film badly shown and this is how we see you. But in seeing and hearing it is at a great distance, it is not clearly audible or visually perfect, for we are working on the field of vibration as we said. It is as if as you were to look across the sea at another island, you would see it but not in great detail! We are not as concerned with seeing and hearing as projecting our thoughts to you in a most clear way for you to understand, so the power of concentration we use is directed through this channel's mind, to your minds and your understanding. It is only when we pass through the vibrational fields from one level of life to another that we see and hear clearly. You may not see and hear us as very often as when one of your loved ones depart you do not see or hear him. He sees and hears you but in a most confused fashion for he does not understand that he has passed the world of the living and is now in the realms of the astral plane and then he can sometimes, become Earth-bound. *We* cannot become Earth-bound, even the choice of that is denied us, for we have passed those experiences and no longer wish to return to that state. We work totally on vibration which creates sound and colour rather than the ordinary ways of hearing and seeing. In that sound and colour can be created a true picture of your identities, but this is another aspect of our communication skills. It is not just *this* group which is working at this moment. This group in a combined way is giving forth words and our knowledge through this channel, but there are others that are working on the vibrations of sound and colour to create a picture."

"Do you understand?"

Soren then said his farewell amid the thanks of the group.

10

HIERARCHY MADE SIMPLE

"It is very difficult when man speaks of the Hierarchy to give you an understanding of what this truly means, for man's imagination can only absorb the words from books and words from others. But to understand that you all are the children of this world and are part of that Hierarchy, it is difficult to bring an understanding to the mind of man with his limited ability to fully comprehend that which Spirit speaks of.

We have spoken of the different levels of communication and man can perhaps imagine this as a ladder at which he ascends to the different levels, but in truth it is not exactly like this. Those of greater wisdom may be walking amongst you now and yet not know they belong to the Hierarchy, because man in his limited capacity cannot accept – even if told – that he is part of this great wonder. There is a reason for this. When man is re-born all memory of that which he was is removed. It is removed through the transition from the initial stage of the physical pregnancy, when the mind, the spiritual mind and the knowledge is removed slowly and the mind becomes fogged and eventually physical.

In your conversations and your extensive discussions, when man uses the profundity of words and confuses his brothers and sisters with his greater intelligence, it may seem to be all very well but Spirit is natural, Spirit is progressive, Spirit is Divine Wisdom and in the little Soul of man are all these qualities. You *all* belong to this Hierarchy but because of the limitations in man's mind you need to be *told* the way in which this is!

That which is of perfection and profound wisdom in total simplicity and acceptance of the Self is the Hierarchy of all the divine beings of the world. You have among you certain descriptions of these various levels, but in truth all levels come from one source, which is the Divine Creator you call God! It *is* similar to when you were discussing a title for this book – "To Little Frogs, Big Frogs are God!" If you understand this it is only because you hold in awe anyone who gives greater understanding to the mysteries of Spirit. These mysteries are non-existent! The esoteric wisdom you speak of is non-existent! For *all* is within the ability of man's own mental capability of truly *understanding* what he is! If man, in his times of stillness and meditative thoughts, considered what he truly *is*, he would be totally surprised and greatly disturbed if the small voice replied that he was God; for man would assume it was a guide of the egotistical class who was trying to encourage him to imagine himself to be greater than his brother, or he would believe it was his own imagination! He would not accept it was the God-voice within that speaks!

One should never hold in awe any other being, whether they are discarnate or incarnate, for you are *all* equal. Understand that as you walk along this spiritual path you are opening doors to which you hold the key. If it were not so that you *had* the ability to grow mentally aware of your own spirituality, you could not open these doors! The world of Spirit to you is full of amazement but to those that dwell in the spiritual realms there *is* no amazement, there is only a sense of progression of the Soul to which man will become, in further lifetimes, totally aware of his true heritage and in recognising that true heritage will realise that it has always been!

You read your books of great wisdom and yet you do not invite your Soul-Selves to read these books with you, and if you did, a greater understanding would come to your mental ability and also to your spiritual growth.

It is all very well that I should speak to you of the Hierarchy, of the different levels, of the greater wisdom that is above your own capability, but it would be of no value other than to your *mental* ability – it would be of no value to your spiritual enhancement and your union with Soul-Self.

We from Spirit are here to identify with you, that which we once were, and in so doing we bring an understanding to you that what we are, so too will you become, and if this was taught you from a higher level than ours you would grow in understanding that you are all there is. By saying 'all there is' it does not mean there is an end to your capabilities in the spiritual sense. As you grow and are still within and communicate with the hidden thoughts within you, the realisation will dawn upon your physical minds that you *are* the ultimate in all that is! In all its majesty and in all its glory. The word 'all' casts a limitation on the great spiritual nature of man.

We could liken the Hierarchy to that of a great departmental store and if you have an understanding how this great store is run then you have a limited understanding of the way in which the world of Spirit is organised. Above each one of us there are others with greater abilities, but *not* greater understanding for what they know we know, and are yet unable to express it in the same form as you are unable to express our greater understanding of spiritual works and ability. You do not as yet understand completely total thought transmission, whereby the whole context of anything that you wished to discuss one to another would be completely installed in your minds. There would be no beginning, no middle and no end to the totality of the transmission of the wisdom, and it would be instant. In the various levels of the Spirit world this ability takes a 'moment's' time in transmitting, whereas when we speak to the man of Earth that same 'moment's' information to be transferred to you would take approximately one, two or three hours at a time. If you were capable of quickening the receiving of such information in your mentality, then you too would be able to transmit your mental communication and your astral and etheric bodies into the world of Spirit with a thought and this is what the Hierarchy consists of.

The wisdom you learn from your books is of no avail in comparison to spiritual understanding. It is only through your Soul that information about the mental ability of its vehicle can enable the vehicle itself to step further into the realms of Spirit. If it were possible for you to be in the presence of those you call the Hierarchy, there would be total chaos in your minds even if you were receptive enough to understand and realise where you were. You would be inundated and in a sense, 'physically' damaged in your astral body to the degree that your mental capability would be unable to stand the assault – for assault it would be!

Because man does not give himself freely to the Soul guidance, he would be in a physical and mental awareness in a world that was totally foreign and governed by those you may term as the Angels. When the Angels show themselves to man, they show themselves in a *limited* form and yet to man's vision they are the most beautiful creatures ever envisaged in his mind, but because you do not see with the eye of Spirit you would only see the beauty of that divine presentation. You would not see the gentleness of the nature and you would not feel the gentleness of the vibration with understanding. If you had, you would realise that gentle nature and understanding came through hundreds and hundreds of physical lives during which that Angel, or advanced Spirit had undergone and suffered enormous stress – not the stress of the physical world, but the stress of seeking the true Soul and of spiritual understanding. Those who have reached that stage which you term as the Hierarchy are those who have suffered greatly in all forms of life, but *not* under the hand of his fellow-brother, but under the conscious mind and the believing heart to attain in short periods the growth he has reached.

It may seem to man that your limited time on Earth of between seventy and a hundred years is a long time .... It is nothing! So imagine how many lives and life's experiences you would have to undergo in continuous torment of the mind and heart before the purification of man through Soul communication, and so it goes on. Slowly you ascend the 'ladder to Heaven'. Man has not even put his foot upon the *first* step, but he wishes to know and be presented the Highest Realms of Spirit he can imagine. If this were possible man would become deranged for he does not have the ability in absorbing all this wondrous information. We ourselves are not so much further up the ladder of evolution, a word you loosely use, than you. In so saying, our ability to just communicate from the level at which we are to the level at which you are, has taken eons of time to perfect and in its perfection is *still* limited!

What do you mean by Hierarchy? Obviously those that know and understand and are greater than yourselves! Understand this, man of Earth, there is no-one that knows more or is greater than man himself, for the God-Spark is in man! It is simply that the God-Spark needs to manifest in its Christ-conscious effort to the conscious mind of man for this God-Spark to be! This is what we are aiming for in the world of Spirit!

FOR GOD HAS RAISED MAN HIGHER THAN THE ANGELS.

There are many, many teachers from our level working with groups such as yours and the information we are giving you, the teaching and the understanding that we are trying to instil in your mind, is being given in various groups all over your world *now!* In your later years you will recollect as you read and begin to communicate with other groups and you will realise you have all been given the same information.

You are a creation of God - we are also that same creation. It is simply that we and others above us are more intelligent, knowledgeable, and more spiritual than you on the physical plane are in your present time. But this shows the *strength* of Spirit that you are walking upon this Earth with the assaults of the physicality's of your Earth, so therefore you are growing – you are reaching your mental understanding of spiritual teaching – and expanding towards that which you term the Hierarchy!

When we sit in our groups of stillness and meditation, our form of communication is not forth-coming as this communication is to you. As I speak, you hear me, as do others with whom we communicate, but when we communicate with those that teach us it is without vocal sound, so is this the Hierarchy? Or is this the fact that we have grown with spiritual understanding and with practiced meditation and are able to accept information and spiritual guidance in silence, or does it mean that those who communicate with us *are* of the Hierarchy?

The desires of man are beyond his capacity to understand. If we have not given you the information that you desired at this point, then you must return to your books of teaching, but in so doing be aware that you are listening also to the voice and the interpretation of man's limited understanding."

"Do you understand?"

Amid thanks and blessings the group agreed they did understand.

Soren then continued:

"We of Spirit endeavour to teach you the way of the heart – the way of joy – the way of total happiness within the individual, and if in our teachings we bring to you an understanding that you are all most precious to the Source from which you came, then our work is although not complete, but satisfactory to ourselves. We do not take pleasure in the sense we are superior, we take pleasure that we are able to give you information and guidance which encourages you and helps you to step further on the path of personal spiritual growth. This is our aim. If you wish a grander, greater teaching of the different levels of the Hierarchy then you must go to those who are concerned only in that field, but they will teach you no more than we ourselves. They will also teach you that it is more important to follow the wisdom in your own heart than the wisdom from your books, for in your books comes sometimes, wrongly interpreted messages that will bring to the mind of man thoughts of grandeur. We are *not* grand – we are *not* superior – we, like you are beautiful, we, like you are most precious, we, like you are on the pathway of Return, but we stop occasionally to teach you, therefore, you stop occasionally to teach others but teach simply, teach with your heart, *not* with your mind, for the mind *will* follow the heart. The mind will learn to communicate with the Wisdom in man's heart and once he does he will then mentally be able to communicate with the Wisdom of the Silent Word and the teachings of the Silent Voice. The Silent Voice is the voice of man:

> Is the Voice of the Soul.
> Is the Voice of the Spirit.
> Is the Voice of that which we call God."
> "Bless you!"

Soren then stated there would be time for just one question, which immediately followed:

"Soren, while you were speaking about the Hierarchy I mentally asked you a question and although you did answer a number of questions, I wondered why you did not answer that particular one. Can you explain the reason why?" questioned Mark.

Soren replied:

"If you wish to know of things other than that of which we are speaking why not communicate with your own guide? It is not always the way of teachers to mentally answer a question from those who attend a class, although it can be done. It is the way of teachers to communicate one to another, i.e. my group would communicate with your group; but as we have told you before if you wish to direct your question to your group they will give you an answer. *If* that group deems it necessary for that information to come via *this* group they would approach us. It is not that we restrict the ability of Spirit, but you asked of the Hierarchy. If you and others from your world should direct their questions to one that has a teacher, can you imagine how overworked we as teachers would be? We each belong to different groups with different teachers and if you seek wisdom, speak to the one that dwells within you – your True-Self, your Spirit-Self that is also your spiritual master. When the time is right the answers will be given."

"Do you understand?"
The group thanked Soren for his teachings.
Soren said, "Then good, thank you and now I will go."

11

MAN KNOW THY SELF

"Very often it is important for man to understand the way of the ancients, and yet in truth man has not changed since those times to the present day. When you speak of man knowing himself, is this not what all teachings from those of the Spirit Realms have come with each time, in each group and in each generation in each of your millenniums; and yet man is hesitant to look within to seek that which he truly is, for he is fearful of seeing both sides of himself. By this we mean man – we do not mean Soul – we do not mean Spirit – we do not mean the God-Spark which dwells within each and every one of you, we simply mean man! Man is a fearful creature and defends himself and those he loves in his selfish manner from any assault from within and without, for within are the means of the greatest assault done to mankind and his fellow beings. How else can you walk this path of spiritual knowledge and wisdom if you do not at first know yourself and in so doing can tread confidently on this path of awareness? Man states that he knows himself and his desires and his wants and yet in his time of loneliness he is desperately aware that beyond him there is a greater aspect – call it what you will – and it is indeed the Soul that dwells within that is the True Self and in knowing Self man knows God.

You speak of your pagan philosophers and the wisdom that they brought forth to the minds of man and yet in those groups of pagan wisdom was also the aggression of man's nature and refusal to be what he truly was, thus preventing him from being that which you call the Christ, which you call the man, Jesus, to bring forth the joy of healing, the joy of sharing and caring. You speak of compassion and we have spoken of compassion before, for compassion is a sister of wisdom, compassion is the sister of man and Self.

In your efforts to be of goodly nature do you not understand that by expressing goodly nature you are using in effect the advice of the pagans that refer to God as good? Do you not understand that by seeking the goodness within yourselves you are helping to bring forth the goodness in others? You are expressing God and you are bringing forth God from the physical being of others! If you understand and have a limited knowledge of wisdom, it is to your benefit as individual men of Earth to seek the Self that *is*, for the Self can be nothing *but!* Man is here for such a short period of time and yet within him the residence of the Soul is broadened through its aspect and understanding and experience of the physical world, and it takes with it into another phase of life all that knowledge and experience of the physical ways of man. Can this disrupt the Soul? It can, as we have spoken before, cause confusion amongst the Soul aspects of God that they become earth-bound and can become dominant and use their intelligence to overpower the man of Earth and rule him in fear, but if man truly knew himself to the depths of that true Soul-Self – that which has been governed and coveted by the desire of man – he would find perfection. He would find compassion in its true sense, and compassion would first be applied to the physical being with the physical being's understanding of joy being the result of discovering his true nature. There have been many, many teachers on your Earth during the time of man seeking God and each of these teachers have stated during their times of teaching for the student to know himself, for the student is not seeking true Self, he seeks that which he thinks he should be and in so doing becomes lost. He does not understand compassion, he does not understand love, he does not understand patience and the virtues of which you so selfishly gather to your selves, for you have given a material understanding to these qualities. These qualities of the Soul are the qualities of the Divine Spirit that breathes life into man. They are the qualities of the aspect of God! If man could enter into the stillness of his being - his being is that of the Soul-Self – he would recognise what true compassion is and would bathe himself in it, realising that he is the creation of the Soul – the Soul being part of that divine you call God, who walks the Earth embedded in that Soul of man. Does it not say, 'Man Know Thy Self' and in so doing KNOW GOD! But man limits himself because he is fearful to tread further into that secret place which is termed the Kingdom of God, which your Christ said is within and where else can it be but *within* the physical form of man. Heaven lies within!

If you read of your pagan philosophers and if you read with the eye and understanding of Soul, you would see the truth in their teachings. Their teachings were simple, but man being 'greater than God' has filled this simple knowledge with the profundity of their intelligence, not understanding that intelligence is limited by man's mind and not by man's Soul, for if it were governed by the Soul the intelligence would be haloed in perfection and all wisdom would come through the intelligent voice of man but based on the simplicity of pure divine compassion. When you help another it is for the exchange of a favour. If one does something for another it is done hoping that favour will be returned. Compassion gives – it asks for nothing, love gives – it asks for nothing, and in truth some of your pagan philosophers and men of today are givers of light and truth, but it is the mentality of man that casts a shadow upon this love and truth. In seeking for enlightenment you do not understand that you are already *in* that state of enlightenment, that within you is the grandeur of the Spark of God, how else can it be? Man spends lifetime after lifetime seeking Self and Self walks with him! It is in the times of your silent meditation when you apply discipline to body and mind that you have a glimpse of the beauty of your True Selves, but in glimpsing this beauty man denies his own recognition and recognises this divine beauty as being outside of him. This cannot be, for in its simplicity, the statement, 'Man Know Thy Self' is that man *sees* Self – that man *is* Self! But man needs identification, recognition – not from others – but of that which he terms 'himself'. Man does not know his True Self and even when you speak one to another of your truths you are not divulging that true expression of the Soul. If you did you would understand that as you allow the Soul to speak through you, you have allowed the Self within to express its Self *with* your knowledge. A combination of minds becoming *One*: Man's mind and Soul mind, for they are separate at this stage of your life, it is not until you seek that inner silence, that inner place when you and Self become one and you portray the True Soul.

Sometimes it is easier for the True Self, the known Self by recognition of man's own intelligence, which begins like the sun slowly rising and casting its brilliance upon the shadows of the Earth – the Soul rises and casts the shadows from the mind of man – and man sees with the spiritual eye that the beauty that dwells within that same Self is within all the physical beings of his world. MAN KNOWS HIMSELF and in so knowing knows God and in so doing sees God in all things. He becomes the Creator under the control and loving discipline of the Soul-Self, Spirit-Self, God-Self and man becomes complete!

You are *all* philosophers in a sense, expressing your own understanding, but the great pagan philosophers knew that as they expressed *their* understanding, it was *also* the understanding of the brothers and the sisters that listened but who, as yet, were unaware of that same knowledge being within them and this is how it is with man today! It is also said 'no man is an island' and yet man *is*, for he has created the little world in which he as an individual exists, and he protects this little world by his selfish action of refusing to see his True-Self. For if he did and became that Self, the little island on which he lives would expand to accommodate all that dwell upon his world, and he would recognise the One-ship that is also there in the form of little Souls, of little Selves.

There is an understanding in the limited knowledge of man that as he identifies with Self so too are the brothers of his world beginning to do the same in varying degrees, but the one that recognises that another has stepped into the unknown region of Self is elevated to a degree of self-satisfaction that an expansion of his True-Self – his Spirit-Self - his God-Self, is emanating through all forms of life!

There are those among you now, as there has always been, who will refuse to see the sun rising in their minds and hearts, and they cast shadows on those that claim to be believers. It is difficult for man to believe in something that he has no experience of, but a true believer is a believer in Self, for in beginning to identify that True-Self, he is expanding his own wisdom and knowledge of both the physical world and the world of Spirit. He understands the relationship and the necessity for the world of Spirit, for the world of Soul, for the world of Self, to manifest in the world in the physical form; and in so happening all men will know their True Selves and in identifying with True Selves recognise it is in totality the *ONE SELF OF GOD!* For we are all God, there is no separation between the most insignificant creature of man or the highest of the astral planes and beyond. We are ONE and we of the higher levels are beginning to understand in reality what our True-Self is and its capabilities. We separate the words for your understanding when we say *we* and *its* as the reality of God, for if we should try to explain who in truth we were, and if we said we were God, and by this, we are also including you, as this Divine Being, would you understand?

Your pagan philosophers in the profundity of their teachings, in truth taught in simple manner, they taught in the language of that time and *yet* they taught as you are now being taught by others of your world. It is simply that you do not understand the wisdom behind the simplicity and when man does, he will realise that the power of God, that which you are afraid to identify with, in all its greatness is total simplicity in life, for you *are* life and despite the complexities of your physical forms, within it lies the True-Self. MAN KNOW THY SELF!"

"Do you understand?"

The group thanked Soren agreeing that they understood and a question was asked about the Akashic records and why they were not available to man to enable him not to repeat any errors that had been committed in the previous lifetime, to which Soren replied:

"If man were to know of the errors in his previous life, would it mean that he would not commit these same errors in *this* life? For the life he is living now consists of different ways of living than a previous life, so therefore the errors made under *certain* circumstances would not apply now, but the *same* errors could be made in this lifetime under *different* circumstances. The reason why man has not been able to see into the Akashic records is simply because he has no understanding of his true reality. If he did, they would be presented to him on request, for he would be requesting this from his *true Soul-Self.* If this information were available to man on this Earth, he would become so absorbed with previous incarnations and trying to analyse the mistakes he had made and how to correct them, then this life would be fully occupied with past lives.

The Soul, in its journey through the different lifetimes of passing through the time barriers from one life in to another, is as we have said before, already progressed, so it is not the Soul that *needs* to progress. Its aim is to awaken man's mind and man's heart in once more understanding again the need to seek the true Self of Soul. There are times in the lives of all men when these records are presented to him, but if you consider the numerous lives that he has led, spanning many thousands of years, can you, with your mental limitations, absorb all the errors with the intent of correcting them? Far better to recall, if it were possible, the good deeds done and to walk the path of goodness than to dwell on errors made in the past. It is not good to dwell in the land of mistakes but it *is* good to realise and understand that man has stepped away from a mistake, whether it can be rectified is immaterial, but if he dwells in goodness and holds that goodness in his heart he would be filled with joy, so therefore, the mistakes once made would *not* be repeated.

God has given man an intelligence, God has given all living forms an intelligence, and it is with this intelligence that the grass and flowers turn towards the sun regardless of the winters to come and the winters gone and this is how it should be for man. Look forward to the opportunity of expanding the natural joy within you, all be it through study, but again we would emphasize the concentration on the joy that is within, and in that joy the ability to be *still* and in that stillness comes the knowledge of the furtherance of man's own growth. The Soul itself does not grow; its progressive state is to teach man that he may manifest God through the tuition of his Soul.

It is difficult for those of us who no longer tread the earthly plane, for our past lives in the Akashic records have been opened to us and we have seen the good and the bad in which we have lived, but we do not dwell in the bad and the dark sides of our lives, and as we progress in a growing understanding *in* understanding that True-Self leads, we as little Souls – totally aware – walk in the path of Spirit! Man, as a physical being becoming aware, is beginning to walk the path of the already progressed Soul – it leads you, it guides you, it becomes part of you. You are brothers, you are sisters as one, and Soul will lead man to the full understanding and wisdom in the mental capacity of the earth-being to be his own Akashic record with understanding, but without the full record being presented. It is for man to move forward and not to dwell in his past! If man dwells in his past he will not go forward in the sense that his True-Self desires and he will then create a problem for himself which will limit his advancement. Seek not that which has *gone* but seek that which always *is*; and as man does he will find that his Soul-Self will become more accessible and when man passes into the world of Spirit and acknowledges his True-Soul-Self, Soul and man becoming one, there will be an understanding of the Akashic records. So therefore, do not be concerned of what man once was and what he has done, be concerned only with what you are and what you will do – and if this is done to the best of man's ability in the light of honest understanding, he will do well!

Do you understand?"

The group thanked Soren again for his talk and asked if they could pose another question concerning Atlantis, its whereabouts and its people. Soren agreed he would speak of what he knew and said:

"Your world is already discovering cities beneath the seas of the world and it is also known that the people of these were very advanced, but man has always wanted to put things in order and has not marvelled over these discoveries and constantly questions them. If you are asking where Atlantis is, I do not know, for your world has changed a great deal since I was there. Atlantis in the broadest aspect of your understanding of the grandeur of this city, of this island, of its people, is limited because of the distortions which have occurred in your world since the time of Atlantis, but in saying it is known that it is in the – the words are different – it is more to the Baltic regions. It is much larger than man believes it to be and it covers many of your oceans in the different levels of cities beneath the sea, but because man is so intent in finding Atlantis itself, he misses the greatness of those other cultures that were there at the same time and shared the same knowledge. What they lacked was control over the individual. They were advanced as a race as were many of your underwater cities and in recent times the Romans and others cultures. Your world has changed drastically and the island on which I was born during one of my lives has been totally obliterated by volcanic activity. There has been discoveries of cities destroyed by volcanoes and by eruptions of your world and distortions of its land, but if you study your ancient maps and made comparisons with your modern maps you would see the similarities as one would a child's jigsaw, each piece connecting with another and if this is so and the world on its axis has altered, then that which man is looking for is towards the area I spoke of. As to where its people are, its people are scattered throughout your world. Some are here, some are there, and it is of no importance. The importance is again the references made to the Akashic records. Has man grown in his heart and understanding any more than he was then, and the answer to that is NO, for man has become more selfish than he was then. Your history books paint pictures of beauty of those they choose to and those that they do not choose to, they do not. Man does not speak with the voice of Spirit."

"Do you understand?"

The possible publication of Soren's teachings as a book was mentioned, and a member of the group asked if Soren would give a brief resume of when he had last incarnated on Earth, and did Soren agree with them that it might be of benefit if this information was made available. Soren agreed and proceeded to talk of a previous lifetime spent on Earth.

"My last incarnation – and there have been many – as I said before, was once on a small island that was destroyed by a volcano. I remember very little for I was but a child. I was born and I was dead. I remember my skin was dark. I remember there were other children and I remember an animal that laid on me but I think that both of us at that point were dead.

If you are referring to the time when I was born as a leper then you will remember that I told you then that my parents and my brothers were also lepers and it was at that time I found that Christ-Self, as man would term it now, but I would not have identified it as a Christ Consciousness for I did not know of the Christ. What I did know was that within the body in which I found myself there was a great beauty, and yet my outer form was hideous. But the beauty I found inside I now know was my Soul-Self. For I questioned my situation and questioned my pain and I questioned the disfigurement and the smell than emanated from my body and I watched my decaying flesh! But it was during those times of immobility, when my legs would no longer support me and I was left in the darkened cave to die, that the light of God shone upon me. I did not know it as God: I simply knew it as a light that brought me comfort. I only knew the sense of vibrations around me when I was lifted from my physical body and the release of pain and yet I still took with me my mental understanding of my deformity.

But for a period of time I lay in a kind of sleep state and it was during that sleep state that I discovered who I truly was and in that discovery I saw *within* that form, the most beautiful creature – it was not of my imagination – I saw my True Self, and I became that Self. I now know that it was my 'Soul Identity' that had presented itself to me through my stillness and my suffering. I was unable to do anything other than think and ponder on the predicament of life and as I learned to appreciate I learned to recognise myself and in so doing I passed into the world of Spirit, whereby I was able to cast the shadow of my former Self away easily for I knew my true identification. As to my age, I was approximately in my young teenage years. I was no longer a child but I was not a man so therefore I passed very young in comparison, and yet to me those years were a lifetime for I was born with the deformities I had. They simply degenerated, but my Soul manifested and I became what I am now. Now I have a greater understanding which has come to me while in the world of Spirit but I have since returned to your Earth planes since that time as a leper. I have lived as a woman, I have lived as a man. I have suffered, I have experienced joy, and all these experiences have been of benefit to me, for as I now reside in the world of Spirit as, I will say, an advanced Soul, I can look back on my victories, for in the past three life times I have succeeded in physical form, to understand, to act as and allow to be represented by my True Self!"

"Do you understand?"

Soren then said it was time for him to leave and thanked the group for listening so attentively.

12

MEATEATERS

There had been a number of times when the group had discussed vegetarianism, and Mark had claimed it was the height of compassion to refrain from consuming the flesh of animals. The group agreed this would be the question presented to Soren at the following meeting. They would also ask if refraining from eating meat would help their spiritual growth.

"Man is the custodian of his world and in so being he is also the protector of the world, and if he thinks that by not eating the meat of the animals of the world he is protecting those creatures he must think again, for man himself is polluting this Earth. Man is creating the hazards within the world and man has experimented upon the animals, upon the world, upon the airs and the seas, for many generations. He has discarded his rubbish in the environment and then bitterly complains about the filth that he breathes and eats and drinks, and if you believe that in just not eating meat you are being compassionate, then this is for you to decide. But remember also your world has a Soul.

There are creatures upon your world that are gradually becoming extinct, and this is not because they are being eaten, but because they have been used for sport, for vivisection, and they have not been taken care of by man. If your world was unpolluted by man's actions, then these creatures would live freely on the same Earth as you and share in its beauty.

We speak of those who say that by denying themselves meat it is to be hoped that eventually this way of living would be accepted by all and compassion would be shown to creatures of the world, but until man can show compassion to *himself* then compassion in *itself* is no use to man or beast. For man can portray compassion as he cares for man on his Earth and the animals that are beneath him, but if he simply shows it by denying himself the flavour of the meat, then he might just as well eat that creature! Compassion is a quality that not only dwells in man but in the beasts of the fields and these beasts show more compassion than man. It is the quality of the Soul that is in *both* man and beast!

The animals of the world kill to eat and man also kills to eat, but man does this killing knowing he is creating and causing pain. He knows he is creating fear in the animal! The animal simply experiences the pain and the fear; it does not understand the cause or the effect of his death. But man, in his approach to the creatures of the world, is still a destructive force and then he turns to the man of science who will create a substitute food which man will eat thinking he is protecting the creatures of the world and he is not, for it is having a diverse effect on the body of man!

If you think of other substances you put into your bodies, meat-eating itself has very little effect. You drink your wine, you smoke your cigarettes, you inhale substances to keep you awake, to make you sleep, you take medication on the advice of your doctors and your medical professionals without understanding what these medications are doing to other areas of your body, and yet you insist that by not killing the animals of your world to eat, you are showing compassion. Man *must* show compassion to himself before he can show *true* compassion to others of his world! He must stand back and survey that which he inflicts upon his own body and in so doing will remove the negativities from his own mind and his own physical being, before he can remove these same things from the minds and the bodies of others.

There will be amongst you for many, many years, people who will eat meat and these will be condemned by those who do not, there will be those amongst you that will drink wines and smoke cigarettes and be condemned by those who do not. You are so busy condemning others for their faults that you do not 'see the log in your own eye,' and that is denial of the Soul. Man in his conscious thinking truly believes that by denying himself the enjoyment of life he is doing that which God wishes, but this is not so. What God's intent is, what Spirit's intent is, what the little Soul that resides within the physical body of man, and its intent is, that man shows peace and compassion and love unto himself *first* and *foremost*. Once man has attained this state of perfection then he will practice the art of compassion by no longer killing his younger brothers and sisters.

There is another aspect of the clear thinking mind which approaches the state of meditation, through which man denies even his own sustenance of the body. This is to create a sense of a light-bearing situation – an altered state of consciousness – within his mind, whereas in fact, because he denies himself sustenance and he is simply without food, there is a vagueness in his mind and in so happening, he reaches another state of altered consciousness. This is all very well, but during this state of consciousness the physical body can suffer. It is as if you were practicing different breathing methods and if one should alter their way of breathing without a controlled method again the physical body would suffer. It takes constant practice and dedication to your chosen path.

It is man during the time of his earthly form who makes his own path difficult. It is for the man of Earth during the time of earthly existence, to act accordingly to the way of his world. What man must learn is the discipline of mind and heart, *not* the physical body! Once the mind and heart is disciplined in the way of the Soul, then these added qualities to the physical being will come naturally – not with the thought that this is good or bad – for it is a natural movement of Soul influence on man's conscious mind and there is no denial or decision to make! If man chooses to deny himself anything that creates discomfort to his physical being and his way of thinking and as such, still endeavours to walk the spiritual path, then these actions are not good for the Soul, for in denying himself man creates a negative vibration which interferes with his ability to be at one – to be still – for the communication with Spirit. Stillness of the mind is a gradual process and it cannot be reached through denial, for while man in denial resents that which he has forsaken, it simply means he is not ready to take that path – that chosen path – made with the conscious mind. It is the influence of the Soul manifestation that brings the purity to mind and heart of man and in its turn will bring about a natural adjustment of his bodily desires. Once this has been attained, man will take action to purify his world, to purify the water he drinks, the land from which he gets his sustenance and his awareness to the Soul that lives within the animal body, and *then* he will no longer be the one that eats the meat of animals. Just because man does not smoke, does not drink, does not eat animal flesh, it does not *mean* that he is filled with compassion and his actions are based on compassion, although he may truly believe this is so, but if in his times of trial the anger that wells up within him in his mind and his heart has shown that the discipline he is mentally applying is not sufficient, for that discipline has not been governed by his desire to worship and act upon, or to become that God we worship!

It is for man to be in the streams of spiritual growth as one with the Soul entity that is within that they walk as *one* on that path and in so doing will bring the qualities of the Soul and *not* the assumptions of man. There is a great difference between the desire of man and the desire of the Soul, although the desire of man may be to project compassion it is not until he can acknowledge the Soul entity as being that of *pure* compassion can man learn to express that same quality.

Man is endeavouring to save the creatures of his world – to save them from extinction – and this is good, for man is beginning to realize that the confines of the caged animal is not good and that same animal should run free in an environment that is good for it, but in so doing man is not allowing total freedom of that animal. The animal is still being governed by man's opinion as to how that creature should be cared for. It may be out of natural kindness of the heart, but it is certainly *not* through the natural compassion derived from the acknowledgment of Soul entity that motivates man's action, but at the same time it does show a growth in man's mind that he should take these actions, for man is beginning to care. But the majority of the world beings are not governed by the will of the Spirit, by the will of the Soul and the will of God. If he were, then indeed, the lion would lay down with the lamb and this is not meant in the sense of the animals but in the sense of man, for man himself is two beings – he is both lion and lamb and it is at times of distress or comfort that he portrays both sides of his personality.

When the lion lays down with the lamb it simply means that man has found the perfected balance within by allowing the Soul influence to guide him. It does not mean man will no longer eat or kill the wild beast, other than the wild beast that dwells *within*, and he will then portray that which is perfect for himself and his world. Man has been given dominion over the world and its creatures, but it is not until man allows these qualities of the Soul to rise within his own heart that he himself will realize his own mistakes. These mistakes will not be sacrifices at this point, it will not mean they will no longer eat meat because it is not good to do so, they will simply *not* eat meat! But until that time man will find substitutes and man will go through a phase in his life when the realisation that the substitutes he is using are not sufficient for his physical needs. When this is discovered, man's physical frame and the use of the physical body will change, man's form will change, his actions with the physical body will no longer be as it is now!

If man is governed by the Soul intent, then the changes which will occur in the physical body will be the *natural* changes governed by the Soul's direction. Man's body will take on a different form which will be more attractive to the eyes of the Spirit. When we say more attractive we do not mean in a beautiful way, we simply mean in the way that the advanced Soul, in advanced physical form, and the display of that form, will be more brilliantly manifested, the body will become perfected! When this perfection happens it will be because of Soul manifestation in accordance with the co-operation of man's mind. The creatures of your world will be looked upon as equals, they will be looked upon as your true brothers and sisters and as you care for your sick and your needy now simply because you are human, you will care for the beasts of your world simply because they are of *your* flesh and you will understand that as you devour flesh you are devouring a physical being of your world and in so doing you are devouring the life force of God!

In some cultures it was, and still is, believed by cannibals that to devour his brother he was devouring his strength, for as you feed your body the strength stays with it. They also believe that as they devour their enemy they were devouring his mental strength and wisdom. This cannot be! Strength can be obtained by eating, wisdom can be obtained by stillness of the physical mind and when wisdom imbeds itself in the mind of man then true compassion will be found amongst the jewels of knowledge.

If man believes that by not devouring meat he is practicing compassion, then that is good, but let man *also* believe that by giving *all* that he is to another in a sacrifice of growing spiritual awareness is a far greater gift to give to another. You are in truth giving your life for your brother, and by life we mean the Soul manifestation, and as you give of your Soul-Self with which you have become *one*, then you are giving back to that other the opportunity to partake of that Soul peace, and he in his turn will learn to manifest that same Soul quality, and as this Soul awareness in your world expands, so too will the true form of compassion be shown not only to the beasts of your world but to the children of your world, the different nations, the different colours and cultures, and compassion will be in the hearts of all men!"

"Do you understand?"

Thanks were extended towards Soren for his talk and a further question concerning the previous incarnations that Soren had experienced to which Soren replied:

"It was agreed there would be a little information of me in the book and this I gave you. I continued to say that the incarnations I spoke of last week were just a few amongst many and if I should give you details and names and places of the lives I have lived, of what use would that be? This book would then not be of harmony and teaching. It is not the lives that man has led that are important. What *is* important is the *result* of these lives. What is important is the harvest man takes into the other worlds and if that harvest sustains your growth in further lifetimes. This is the incentive for the Soul to manifest again and again: That it may begin to establish itself in physical form and thereby manifest God in physical form.

The aim of all Souls is to return again to the physical world to harbour again these physical experiences, but for the spiritual growth itself to come through the form of man and not Soul, for the Soul is already fully grown. Soul is an aspect, a manifestation of God, and as man grows in a Spiritual sense and allows this manifestation of God, *man himself* has allowed this manifestation of God to come into the world.

But to return to your question of my previous incarnations, I will not speak of the lives I have led. I have given you sufficient!"

"Do you understand and agree?"

It was agreed that there would be no more questions concerning Soren's previous incarnations and another question was put about the group of which he was part and did it consist of his Spiritual Family?

"We are *all* part of the Spiritual Family for we are all *ONE* in that family. In our completeness we are a manifestation of God, but the group you speak of – my group – inasmuch is *singular* in its movement amongst you as another group.

But in the combining of wisdom and interest we bring forth the beginnings of a *new* group of which not just us, but you and other groups and their pupils combining as *one* to enlarge an already existing group, thereby *this* group – my group – and another group and their pupils, and so on. As we accumulate and grow we will gather together and become one and so forth. Each group accumulates vast numbers in its growth and in so doing becomes joined with another. Thus the Family of God becomes – but in so saying this – there are aspects of groups, such as ours, who will send forth new teachers from that group to gather around them new aspects through which another group can be formed.

As we divide and separate we also gather and come together as we expand and grow. This group of which I am part not only works with you, this group has sub-divisions, so there are many of us, but as we work with you we number seven."

"Do you understand?"

The group thanked Soren once again for his interesting information and agreed it was time to close the meeting.

13

ENLIGHTENMENT

A question was asked concerning Enlightenment and the Great Invocation.

"When you speak of the Enlightened Ones it is for you to understand that these Enlightened Ones are those who have knowledge – who have *Knowing*. And when you speak the Great Invocation, the Enlightened Beings already know that Christ walks the Earth, that the light of God is already in the mind of man and his Divine Love is also in the mind of man; and the Enlightened One on *Earth* knows this. On your world at present are these Enlightened Ones and they are not from different spheres, different galaxies or on different planes in the furtherance of life. They are with you *now* as they have *always* been!

During the time of prehistoric man, these Enlightened Beings have dwelt upon your Earth and yet in their understanding, the knowledge they had was limited by *man's* knowledge of earthly things. Man as a physical being was not interested in his Soul, or the Spirit, or God in an aware state, but it does not alter the fact that the *knowing* of all things still dwelt within the form of man, within the being of man in his heart and his mind.

But if man speaks of the Enlightened Ones in total awareness of their *own* knowing then these men are few. It is not until man realises that within *him* is his own Christ Being will the understanding of this true knowledge manifest. But man, in his actions towards his brothers of the world in which he lives, is far greater governed by more spiritual thought now than it ever has been, but the light within has not enlarged his way of thinking towards his *own* progression. By progression we mean the progression of man's mind, *not* the Soul within! The Soul is already an Enlightened Being and as we have said many times it is for that Soul to awaken the same knowledge and Spiritual understanding in the mind of man. So therefore, each and everyone that lives upon this Earth must begin to understand that *he*, the man, is an Enlightened Being! This may be difficult to accept for man believes it is the Soul alone – the Spirit alone – God alone, that is this Enlightened Being, but without the form of man this true Enlightenment cannot be made manifest in the God sense or the Christ sense without man's mental co-operation in realising he *is* the Christed One!

There is in your Book a saying which is, "Many are called, but few are chosen!" Do you understand this simple statement? Many of your Earth beings are attracted to various followings of various teachers of the way to God and yet man is governed by the rules made by man! If he allowed his Heart-Self - his True Self - that centre in which all wisdom lies to inspire him, he would walk the path of Spiritual Enlightenment. He would become aware of his own True Nature and not separate himself from Soul but to become One with Soul, realising as a babe recognises its parent as one to whom it gives respect and knowing that parent will guide him in his footsteps on Earth, then man will look to his Soul, his Spirit, to his God to guide him. The man becomes the child!

But man is also his own guide! Man has the key to the doorway to Self-awareness and he holds the key to enlightenment, and once he allows this truth to manifest in his conscious mind he will come to the realisation that he is and has always been the Enlightened One.

You seek your teachers and gurus and a religion to follow and to be guided by, but man in his *own truth* to his conscious mind – that which is of love and gentleness in his heart – follows the path of his heart and will become aware of his True-Self and again in so doing will become and recognise his position among the Enlightened Ones. If we take this further, the Enlightened Ones of those you speak are on the various levels in the Spiritual Realms – they have journeyed the distance of man. They have walked the same path as man and in their realisation as they come to the end of particular paths, begin to understand as a true creation of the Divinity that *is* within *him,* he has been created for the manifestation of that which you term God and in his realisation another stage of enlightenment is reached. It is not a state that is reached in one journey of life, it takes many steps for true enlightenment in the degree that it can be accepted within the limitations of man's mind and to Become! In its Becoming, man then in his conscious thinking and his knowledge of his connection with ONESHIP, and his total enlightenment to the conditions in which he finds himself, his view of the world will be entirely different than it was before he undertook the journey!

He will look upon the world as that which has been created *for* him but *by* him and we mean the Soul entity, the Spiritual connection and the God Presence within. It has been created by the True-God-Self for the manifestation of the Enlightened Being which is the man of Earth!

The enlightened Ones have realised this situation and in their understanding appreciate the fact that the work that has been undertaken by the God-Self has been for the benefit of man in physical form who will eventually come to realise his True-Self. Him being the creator of all things and the Spirit guide of all thinking beings and the Soul that is in all living forms including the physical body of man – for man *is* God - God *is* man – God is in all things and all things are God. For remember, "THE FATHER AND I ARE ONE!" Christ's words!

When one understands this then the enlightenment that man seeks will be open to the understanding of man, but it takes aeons of time and lives before man in true recognition of his Self becomes aware of this Truth and in his awareness becomes an Enlightened Being. His reaction towards his fellowmen and the Earth upon which he lives, changes his view on the aspect of life around him, for in his growth he realises that others are also in various stages of growth and realisation. It may well be that your brother is behind you in his mental growth and understanding – it may be your brother is ahead of you in his mental growth and understanding, but eventually all truth will dawn in the mind of man and *this* is Enlightenment!

The Enlightened Beings of which you speak are those who came to your world and other worlds to bring this understanding and when you reflect back upon this lesson you will understand the simplicity of this teaching. You will realise that as you look back on these early days of the youth of your mentality – the youth of your imagination and the youth of your intellect - you were as yet, not fully grown. Man, in his longing to return to the state of Soul awareness, endeavours to attach himself to a belief that has been taught by men who are not fully conscious of the True-Self and he will follow in spiritual blindness that society or denomination on which he has decided, but in his stillness and in his solitude – for he will suffer solitude, and if he is conscious of his true need for Soul awareness he will seek deeper and deeper within himself!

We can only be signposts and advisors, but those who come from the Spirit Realms do not, in their true growth, tell you to follow one denomination or another. We can only teach you to follow the truth in your heart for in your heart you cannot lie to yourself, for the heart governs all truth, whether they be of a Western or Eastern belief of your world or other beliefs of your world, it matters not! Your Heart-Self does not belong to the world of man, it is the form in which the Soul resides that needs to be encouraged on the path of Enlightenment, and in your stillness these truths and teachings will come.

'But', you say, 'we heard the voice of Spirit from others who sit for us or we hear the voice of Spirit from within our own minds', and this is true, but again I repeat, we are only the signposts, we can point you in the right direction but it is for you to step upon that path and in so doing be governed by the belief that lies within you! You can discard at any moment in your life that which you feel is not true for you and follow another road. It matters not, for eventually, if you are true seekers of truth, you will step upon the path of Enlightenment and when you do your previous attitude to truth will not be, for truth in man's way of understanding will no longer exist. What will exist will be a knowing and in this knowing you will become aware you are an Enlightened Being. This can happen in this lifetime if you persevere on your path.

What is your path?

Your path is a road of True Dedication.

Your path is a road to Self-Knowledge.

Your path is the road to that which you already *are.*

An Enlightened Being!

When you speak of the Enlightened Beings, what is it in your imagination you see? You may see an ethereal being full of light and compassion – full of love and mercy, but you too are all these things, but they are hidden beneath the veil of materialism and man's ego, for man is afraid to show his true, gentle, Self.

In gentleness there is great strength, for gentleness governs anger – gentleness governs reaction towards others' negative actions and thoughts against you. Their reactions can be dismissed easily by your now spiritually aware mind which has followed the path of the heart because it has become enlightened by the true thought of Spiritual growth. So therefore, when a man slaps your cheek, you can turn the other because the first slap will have no impression and neither will others that may follow. It is because you are now governed by Enlightened thought and actions, and others will see this light-change within you and their reaction may be that of confusion or anger or admiration or a need to draw closer to you, so then you would be judged as an Enlightened Being by those who are not yet aware of their True-Selves.

You look upon us from the world of Spirit as Enlightened Beings and we teach you the simplicity of life and in your understanding it seems you need to gather about you greater knowledge from others and from books. This is not necessary: man can find a true relationship with the God within even though he may even be illiterate. It does not take great knowledge and many words for man to truly understand his God-Self.

When man understands this in his heart, where all Wisdom is, his mind will follow, for his mind will be governed by the gentleness of which we speak. It will not become agitated by the actions of others. It will not create within itself the argument against the other and in the mind becoming gentle it controls the emotions of man. The Solar Plexus which is part of the Chakra System or Energy Centres, of which many of you have been taught, is the largest Chakra within your bodies and this is because man has not allowed his true Heart-Self to expand to the degree that it must to govern the mind, and the heart releasing that true potential of Divine Love will correct the disturbances within the Solar Plexus. This expansion of the Heart Chakra will eliminate your emotions that are governed by anger and hate. With this under control it will also govern the physical body, because when man becomes calm the ailments he has suffered will no longer be. There will be no need to take the excessive amount of medically applied drugs on which man depends so greatly in these particular times. He will govern and heal his own body and the bodies of others by his own true enlightenment gained from the wisdom of the heart, which governs the thinking process of the mind and in its turn the emotional outbursts which are created in the Solar Plexus.

It is now the time for the Heart Chakra to play a major role in the spiritual growth of man and this is happening in your world *now*. The number of people who have stepped upon this particular path is numerous and far more that this small group here tonight can appreciate at this time. They are developing in countries which are suffering great hardships and yet they are borne bravely by these heart seekers. The awakened beings are in all classes of life from the rich and the famous to the poor and the unknown. It matters not on the degree of your lifestyle, the pathway to your God-Self is open to *all* men!

We whom you regard as Enlightened Beings have walked your path before you and with you, and when you have grown to a degree when you can recognise the true teacher within yourself, we will then teach other students and so will you in your turn. You are the Enlightened Beings developing into *knowing* Enlightened Beings to achieve to the degree of the saintly beings that you refer to as the Angels of God. You will become part of that Hierarchy of which we spoke a few weeks ago – because you *are* already!

If man could cast away his material desires and wants and make his priority the desire of his Soul-Self, the Soul would manifest in a conscious way to man's mind, its True Enlightened Self and your True Nature would come as a light into your world!"

"Do you understand?"

Once again the group thanked Soren for his inspiring lesson and continued with a question about the Moldavite Meteorite that fell to Earth approximately 14.8 million years ago. It was stated elsewhere that the Moldavite Meteorite came from the Pleiades system and information concerning it and its effects had been channelled by three other mediums. Could Soren confirm this information?

Soren continued:

"The Moldavite Meteorite consists of all I have spoken about the past few months but with the exception of the human Self. Within that stone are the aspects of spiritual growth and it was not by accident it was directed to your world all those millions of years ago. It was a deliberate action on the part of those more intelligent than you. It was known that man would not discover it until many, many generations had passed and during that time the stone, like other stones, has collected unto itself all that is of the world, but the stone itself initially was impregnated with intelligence. Not an intelligence that would be described as of the physical world, but an intelligence that would gather to it only that of positive action. Therefore if it should fall into the hands of one of negative thought then its reactions to those negativities would become reactive in the state of being unable to bring forth that which is positive within it, it would simply shut down. But if any part of those stones should fall into the hands of a man of true spiritual protection and true spiritual directed thought, then the stone's response would activate an action within that man and he could become a true healer in the true sense of the word. Also within it are the properties which, if applied and used under the guidance of an enlightened being, could cure all ills *including* the illness of cancer! But it is more beneficial to eliminate negative aspects of man if used by a man of positive thought.

In your world great trust is put upon the gems, stones and crystals, but man 'feeds' these stones with that which he believes is good for mankind. If man allowed these stones to react in the way that they have been programmed by beings of a higher intelligence than his, then the effects would be far more substantial.

If you should speak to another who knows far more than I do of these aspects of God's other creations you would further your understanding, but in your world there are many stones and crystals and gems that are being wrongly used by man and their power is becoming less and less. If man followed his heart without the influence of the different denominations in the world, and allowed the crystals, stones and gems to follow their own true potential, it would be these stones which would teach man! It would be these stones that would divulge the information of the ages to man's minds. Within each is a recording of its world, the space from which it came and indeed more information of your own world. Information of greater knowledge from beings with greater knowledge than man has been programmed into these stones, and knowledge of other worlds would be made accessible to you.

Now, I do not know if what I tell you is the same as you have read about concerning the Moldavite meteorite particle, but what I will tell you is that all things that come from outside your system were originally part of that to which you belonged. You are aspects of each and every stone and meteorite that enters and is upon your world. You consist of all these elements and man uses them as extensions of his own being. So therefore all that you are can be manifested or transmitted into these stones. The difference with the Moldavite stone is that it repels negativity and manifests positive-ness."

"Do you understand – have I made myself clear?"

The group thanked Soren and agreed on the clarity of his teaching and information. It was decided the time had come to close and they said they were already looking forward to the next meeting.

14

AND NOW TO THE FUTURE

"Very often in the world of Spirit we take time to listen to the chatter of men and they are unaware that we are close by their sides, but we are not constantly at the sides of your people. The Guardian Angels who walk with you are not always with you, but there are numerous companions who in taking the Angels' places occasionally, collect information and report this to the Guardian Angels and we begin to understand the emotional aspects of man, and eventually we, as well as the man of Earth, will take our places within the Hierarchy, for we are *all* part of the same!

And now to the future! What is the future other than that which is always present with man, and yet man does not truly understand this simple fact! When man speaks of the future he speaks of the time when his world will either be annihilated by man's own hand, or the angels who, under the direction of God, will walk upon your world to destroy, and neither of these descriptions are for your world!

Your world will change as man changes and your world will become more *internal* and not *external* as it is now. Man will live *within* the surface of his Earth but he will also live *beyond* the surface of his world, but not in the form that he is today, for there will come to your world another race of people who will unite and mingle with your own and become a new race of man but you will have a similar appearance of man but with a higher intelligence. Your children will be born with that intelligence which will come to the surface of your lives in a short time. That time will not be before our time of return. So when you speak of future you cannot envisage as to how your world will look. It may be during that time of your new world you will return and when you do, this change of appearances will be totally natural to you. But you will return with the forgetfulness of man's mind as it is now, but he will have gained a higher intelligence because of this interbreeding with another race of beings, as it once was in the past. Your Book teaches the world will end, but it will *not* end, for the world cannot end. The world itself has a Soul – a living force – and this force is the property of God. It is part of God and of his creations. Again we can only say, how is it you envisage God? Do not give God a personality. Do not give God the emotions and the thoughts of man – for God is not this! God is as *nothing* but from this God came *everything!* God is that which you term as LIFE and LIFE everlasting – AND LIFE IS GOD – for life that is God and is the creator and the destroyer and is unending!

When we speak of God as the destroyer, he is *not* the destroyer of worlds or beings. It is man with the God Energy within him who becomes the destroyer, and it is through man's foolishness in believing the energy within his own being belongs to man and is created by him. But as your new world grows in the wisdom of the new race that the world will produce, then the understanding of protection will truly form itself in the mind of man. This may seem fearful to the man of today, but if you understand the way of life, the way of Spirit, the way of God, that *is* the Soul entity within you, then that entity will remain the same, even though beings from other worlds will come to your world. The Soul-entity in each one of you, being the creation of that Divine Being you call God, will be exactly the same, but it will be that those physical beings who come from another world will be more intelligent that you, the 'Earthman'. When the combination of these two world entities become *one* in the new form of man, the Soul entity will not be usurped by those from the different world for the Soul entity is exactly the same! As we have said repeatedly before, it is not Soul-progression – it is man's progression – the man of Earth and the man of other worlds!

As to the destruction of your world, it is said the destruction will be caused by fire and not water as was once believed, but it is the fire of man's greed which will destroy *in part* your world – man will adapt and man will learn by his own mistakes and his own pain, but amongst the men of your world who suffer, will also be the LIGHT MAN and he will be the man of progressive understanding on the need of the survival of truth. *Not* of the physical body but the Soul truth within that physical body.

Man in his nature is a survivor – he is a fighter – his animalistic nature rises to the forefront of his actions if he is endangered, but it is the Soul quality in him that will lead him to think clearly on the survival of his self and his world and this will be through the result of *part destruction*. The *part destruction* will cause a re-alignment of the countries of your world. Whereas in the past man has divided your countries and separated your peoples, it will be an upheaval caused by man and *not* the movement of the world which will eventually integrate your countries, and your peoples will no longer have separate identities, and your world then will consist of the combined colours of your world. There will not be black, white, red or yellow, you will be of one colour, one nation united and this will be when your world will be visited by those who will be of similar appearance as yourselves, but of a greater intelligence. The combination will be good and of benefit to the Earth man!

But can you imagine how long this will take? It will not be in your lifetimes or the generations to come. The movement between the destruction – in part – of your Earth and the realisation of wisdom in man's mind will take aeons of time, and this book which we discussed earlier will be lost and so will many other teachings from the world of Spirit, but it matters not, for the banner of life, of love, of constant living life the way that God would instruct man will be and will come to the forefront of man's mind, for he will be guided in joint understanding of his Soul-Self.

Man will recognise that he is simply the conveyer of all that is good and in this will come to the conscious mind an understanding, and he will be at one with his Conscious-Self and his Soul-Self. The total change in man will be of benefit to him and it may seem to the reader at this time of your life that this way of change would be unacceptable to you, for you are used to being as you are. But in your past the world was not as it is today and yet as time passed you became used to being man of Earth, so therefore it stands to reason as the future unfolds and changes of your world and its people occur, you will also accept these events! The same acceptance by the children of future generations will happen at the part destruction of your world, knowing despite this disaster, they survived! Man is made to survive, to enable the Soul entity to complete its journey and to bring home the conscious being in true understanding.

Now to *your* futures, and how do you envisage your futures to be? Is it you will come to an understanding and recognition from others, or is it that your understanding and growth will be of benefit to yourselves? It is wished by those of us in Spirit that your understanding will be of benefit to yourselves and in quiet ways you will influence others who come onto your pathway. It is all very well to have grand ideas, and if you can fulfil these grand ideas to the betterment of Self and others then that is good. But if it is simply for the glamour of communicating with those of us from the Spirit world then this is of *no* benefit to you and each individual must learn this so that when he looks into the future and can envisage the beauty of how this world will one day portray itself, he can be pleased that he had played his small part. For each man must play a part in the progression and beautifying of his own world and his own Self. For as you grow in Spirit you become more beautiful, you become – in your terms – the Guardian Angels of future generations.

As to the future of your Churches and those who govern you, there will be two governing bodies of your world. There will be two races of people joined as one to become One. Your Churches will fall as they are recognised now and the Church of Spirit will be standing upon your world and those that teach the way of Spirit will lead in the same way as the Masters who have been with you in the past – who are with you now – and who will be with you in the future. When you begin to understand the simplicity of this then you will become familiar with the true way of Spirit. You will be drawn onto Paths of Initiation and be led onto the Path of Physical, Mental, Emotional and Spiritual Growth and become walkers on the path of Spirit. All men of your world will become familiar with that which you term the Esoteric, for Wisdom is already in your minds and it is for you to study the way of Spirit to unite in the way of your Spiritual guidance and all that is of mystery and magic and all that is necessary for man to progress. When you become aware of this new frame of mind being your inner knowledge that has always been, *then* will come the changes in your world, because the black evil of your world and the white supremacy of love and the Divine Entity within you will collide, and this is *when* the part destruction of your world will be!

There will be the groups who will practice the Black Arts and be successful. There will be those who practice that which you term the White Art and they too will draw unto themselves successes, but the time will come when the White Light of God – that which is Good – will shine throughout your world. Will there be death and destruction? There *will* be death and destruction! There will be pain and anguish, but also there will be joy and laughter. When Spirit and Soul and the God-Self become awakened in man, then true realisation of man and world survival will be!

This as we have said will *not* be in your lifetime. It is simply murmuring in and around your world. You are being observed by another world and your world is being looked upon as a place where others can live and it is known by us of Spirit and those from Higher Spheres than us, that when this union comes it will be a union that is agreed by both worlds. The man of Earth will not be subjected to force, but he will welcome these alien forces who are similar and from a similar star system, but whose world in its way, is dying and this must be for the worlds to unite in physical form. As one world dies another is becoming altered ready to accommodate those from the other world. Your world is being prepared for such an event but it will be man's negativity that will create most of the pain in your world for man is one that would gather unto himself the riches, but again negative aspects must be for man to recognise his true potential to a more positive life and love. So *all* that happens is *meant* to happen to enable those from other worlds to join you on this Earth to increase your understanding, to improve your worldly gifts, and to give all men the opportunity of a union with men of a far greater intelligence, and eventually Wisdom and Love will be the Law of Man!"

"Do you understand?"

The group thanked Soren for his wonderful insight of the world to come and went on to ask a question. Soren said there would be time for one question because if he gave the young man who asked the questions, 'free reign', he would be there all night!

The group were interested to know if the book was reaching its completion, to which Soren replied yes it was and the book would be completed within the month.

Mark then came in quickly with another question in which he asked, "Is this to be one of the last chapters in the book then?"

Soren said, "The final chapter in this book will be based on Wisdom, but far different to the very first chapter based on the same subject."

Mark then went on to ask if he could put forward another question, to which Soren replied good-humouredly:

"If it is what man would refer to as 'a quickie' then, yes!"

"Soren, you speak of other worlds and you are obviously familiar with our mode of travel and could you tell us how you are

able to travel from one point to another? Could you please expand upon this?"

"We live in the *space* between worlds. Those of us who are from a few levels above the Astral Plane, which consist of forms similar to those of the physical world, live in the spaces between these different worlds and planes. Although we have *form* in which our Spirit-Soul resides, that form is on such a high frequency of vibration, as not to be seen.

As man begins to pass through space he will become aware of passing through areas that seem to be dense. He will pass through areas that may appear to be to him as though he were travelling in the sea. He may also pass through areas which consist of sound emanation through the sound-frequencies of his spaceship and these are the places in which we live. To us they are as real as your world is to you, but if we wish to travel we travel by thought! We simply *think* to be in a place and that is where we are! This is a totally natural procedure of journeying in our way of living. We do not move as man would imagine our movements to be. Our bodies are not as man would imagine them to be! Our bodies are finer and they are, as you would describe, as 'wisps of smoke,' but within that 'wisp of smoke' is an *entire being* and we are this!

We are individual 'wisps of smoke'. The whole of our understanding – our Spiritual growth – are in these forms. If we wish to communicate one to another we simply *think*. This procedure only occurs after *many, many* passages of time as beings, whereby we become one with that which you term the God-Head. The God-Head being a form of *mist-like,* but within this mist is the entirety of all that is known and is intelligent, and we are all *aspects* of that – it is what you may term "The Universal Consciousness". It is *not* the *TOTALITY OF GOD!"*

"Do I make myself clear?"

"Yes, thank you Soren. It was most fascinating and made so clear. We thank you again for coming and look forward in anticipation to our next meeting. Thank you again and goodbye."

15

PATIENCE

"You are as little children awaiting Christmas. When we spoke of the final chapter of this book being based on "Wisdom", in your eagerness it seems that you wait thinking this chapter will accumulate into your minds all that is wise and good, but this is not so. Children do not understand the work and effort and worry which go into the preparation of the festive time for them. It can be compared to the Basket of Golden Fruit, which you hope to accumulate and you do not realise that before you can collect the Harvest of Golden Fruit the land has to be prepared, and this is what we from Spirit have come to do. The 'land' we speak of is in the body of man – within his physical mind and heart – in which rests the seed which with effort will lead him onto the path of spiritual knowledge! For man needs to allow himself to listen to the Voice of the Soul, to teach, to encourage and to guide him on his Spiritual Path!

It takes aeons of time in the preparation of the Soul before it is able to take upon itself the form of man and in so doing he becomes the teacher. He, or It, takes on the role to teach the men of Earth to become awakened to the natural life that is within and this life consisting all of which you term to be God and yet again, aeons of time will pass before you have even a small measure of understanding of what this God is. As we have said before, we in the realms of Spirit are as yet unable to say to you exactly what God is!

We know and we teach that God is a life-force. We know and we teach that God is the Breath which enables you, as a physical being, to live upon your world. The Soul which governs each physical body has been prepared from the Source of Life, the Source of Love and the Source of all that is magnificent, to take this journey in the schooling of man. As you teach a child to be patient and to wait for that day of pleasure and excitement to come, we endeavour to teach man also to be patient in his life-journey!

It is said that 'Patience is a Virtue' and this is what is lacking in the physical attributes of man and yet it is *within* his Soul for it *is* a virtue of the Soul! The Soul, in its endeavour to teach man the way of the Spirit, will try to draw man into that realm of patience, of stillness, of controlled disciplined thought. It is believed that the mind cannot be stilled but it *can*, and in following the direction of the Soul this state of mind can be reached by all those who seek to walk the path of knowledge and wisdom. When we speak of the virtues of Spirit, whether they be of Wisdom, Joy, Patience, Stillness *and* Mental Action, it is to these steps that man takes in his effort to become aware of his True-Self, but man at this time of his spiritual development is limited by his conscious mind-strength which will resist that which is termed as temptation to approach and enter the unknown, and yet we from Spirit would teach you that this Path is the true path of spiritual awareness.

You read your books in which you will find the words of man trying to express the way of Spirit and this is impossible. We, as we use your words, find it difficult to express the True Way of Spirit, the truth of the Spirit and the Joy of the God Entity that is in you!

During your times of material joy there is an uplifting of your heart and there is a lightness of mind and this is an element of God joy, but because of the need to be awakened to the materialism of your world as part of your growth, you do not understand it also to be part of God; if you did you would be able to rest in this state of joy constantly, despite the assaults of the physical world. The greatest assault on man is *by* man, for by his exploring the world of Spirit through his books and speakers, he neglects to understand that he is only on the fringes of the steps that lead to understanding and he is reluctant to step into that so-called dark place!

If man disciplines the mind in true meditation then that which he will envisage will be the true action of the Spirit. This is why your meditative states should be of concentrated effort. Once mind control is, then that which you will see and hear will come from the Higher Spheres of Spirit. If in your stillness you are lax in mental discipline then that which you will see will be simply trickery brought to you by those of the lower levels. This does not mean that clairvoyance from the man of Earth is not true – it is! It does not mean that the healing energy that comes through man is not genuine, for it is, but man on his spiritual journey towards enlightenment must learn discipline for *man's* development. If the *need* is there for rituals, then so be it! If the need in your thoughts is *not* for ritual then so be it – it matters not! What matters *is* the stillness and that the desire in you is genuine! Man must constantly question the actions he takes towards his Spiritual Path. In saying this, am I saying those who simply follow faith without spiritual realisation must continue to do so? No, it simply means that man needs to be governed by mental discipline and visualisation of a choice in which the Soul will integrate in that visualisation, and the words from Spirit which the Soul will endeavour to impinge these truths on the mind of man, and if it is for spiritual progression this method will be successful. If it is simply for the glamour which you term Spiritualism, then it is not good for the Soul that works with you and it is certainly of no benefit to the mind of man. If and when man in his truth and his mental understanding disciplines himself to the way of Stillness, he will accept that these gifts will have no advantage at all unless he is at One with his Soul-Self and *then* these gifts will be acceptable to Soul-man as part of his naturalness of Spirit and your miracles will occur in Soul-Manifested-Man!

The words you speak will be words of truth for it will be the Soul that speaks through you, but with the joint understanding of that of which the Soul speaks, for you have become Soul-man and no longer Animalistic-man who simply takes personal pleasure from that which he can draw from the world of Spirit, for he has now become *part* of the world of Spirit though he walks in physical form upon the Earth-plane!

Man in his worldly experience yearns to take the home-ward journey – that which he terms as Heaven, but Heaven does not exist in the way man understands. Heaven indeed is an act of the heart and the mind and of total Soul-awareness. This heavenly state is with the man of Earth even though he may be under great duress during his physical life. In his joy and realisation man is strengthened physically, mentally and emotionally, for he is aware that his strength is that of the Spiritual-Self, and in the realisation of these strengths becoming One he will truly understand the words of your book – "that you are of Earth and you are of Spirit". There is no division in man-Soul mind and there is no separating, or of acting different characters into different situations. Your personality in union with Soul growth becomes a natural procedure in presentation of Soul-man and the personality drops away as of nothing.

Man at present thinks if he gives himself freely to the Soul impression he will lose his identity, but he *cannot* lose his identity for he has always been in a Soul manifestation. What is lost is the physical identity you, yourself recognise, but as you grow more in spiritual understanding this is of no loss. It is as though you had cast the scales from your eyes and you now see that which is of the truth!

When we refer to you as excitable children it is simply because, as a small child learns to walk it has to learn with measured step to keep its balance, and man in his thirst for knowledge from his books and the words of others takes seemingly great leaps in his limited mental capacity but within that mind-memory there are divisions - there are questions and there are spaces which cannot be fulfilled by the written or spoken word. The spaces within the mind of man can only be fulfilled if he sits in quietness and if he disregards the rush of the earthly happenings around him, for spiritual progression. This spiritual progression is not necessarily on a weekly basis as man is influenced into believing – it becomes a *daily* act – it becomes a *living* thought in his mind. This does not prevent him from the actions of the Earth but it does indeed, strengthen him, for the mind becomes clear. The mind becomes able to absorb all that it has learned. The mind becomes the Book of Man and the heart is the Hall of Wisdom.

There is a theory that if one should lose the organ you call the heart and it is replaced by another, that one would be influenced by the donor, but nothing *can* be lost! For within the heart-centre of man is still the Wisdom of Spirit for all centres are within all men, so therefore, that which you lose can be gained from an action of man. When man's original heart becomes defective and is replaced by another it is thought that he takes on that other's personality. This cannot be, for if man is true in his spiritual path he will remain upon it, for he has opened the door to Wisdom and although we speak of the heart being the home of Wisdom it is the heart-centre which is situated near the physical organ of the heart. It is something that cannot be held in human hands. It can only be searched for and found by the human mind, for the mind also is not a *physical* organ – it is not a collection of muscles and such, as is the brain. The mind is that of space which is filled with thought whether it is thought of material effect or that of the spiritual influence – it is the Soul at work, and in that space is true spiritual understanding of the pathway man must take to become Soul-Man. This is the division within man of which we speak, so understand when we speak of this division it cannot be a division as man would understand it to be, for it is *part* of man, and it *is* man. It is the Soul within which influences the mind of the potential Soul-man.

Man is influenced by the outward ways of the world and in this influenced state of mind he can encourage or discourage the movement of the Soul. The Soul will still supply within that space of man all that he needs to become successful in the world, but until man opens the door to the heart and learns to discipline his mind and control his wayward thoughts then he, in a conscious state, cannot walk upon the Spiritual Path.

But do not let this defeat you in your journey upon this path for no matter how many times you tell the child that time of joy, that time of pleasure, the time for the presents, is not for a long period, it does not alter the child's excitement and lack of patience and expectancy, and you yourselves must learn patience and remain in the expectant state. It is knowing that your Soul-Self and your physical self are One and on the day of joy when your physical, conscious mind awakens to this fact, the door to the heart opens. Wisdom will be yours!

When we speak of the qualities of the Soul, can you not accept that these qualities are the natural part of man's growth? It is feared by him during his life on this Earth, as a personality that he will – as a physical form – become as nothing, but in the union with Soul and the conscious mind comes the true realisation of what he is, what Soul has endeavoured to do which is to manifest the Christ, the God, the Buddha and all those you refer to as your God, upon this Earth; and man – as the child – will be filled with the conscious joy to the fact that he is a True-Spiritual-Being. His path then will be to manifest that True-Self in the world!

He will not lose his identity as an Earthly being when he passes into the second or the third and so forth, planes, but he will gladly leave off that coat of the physical form for all that he has learned and understood will be carried onward in his True-Soul-Self.

Once man recognises the true Soul-Self residing in physical form, the union of his memories, his joys, and his experiences will continue for a period of time, and all that he has experienced in *this* life will be part of man's growth in the *next* life. There will be no memory as such, as to *whom* he was, but *all* that he was will go forward into the next incarnation. You are Souls encased in physical form!

What we are trying to say is that you the Soul has chosen the physical form in which you live to manifest the True-Self through the form of man, and in so doing bring that which you term the Christ Consciousness into fruition and the God of all things to walk this Earth, and this the Basket of Golden Fruit – this is your Harvest! Your riches will be of the Earth and the Spiritual realms. The Soul in physical form will bring all that is beneficial to your Earth and your brothers and sisters of the world.

It is difficult for us of Spirit to help man to understand that he is a Divine Being in Soul form encased in physical form. When this realisation dawns on the conscious mind you will then begin to realise that those of us that come to teach are *ONE* with you! We as groups of spiritual teachers and you as students of the Earth, as we discuss that which we refer to as God, realise that we, as *ONE* complete Being are God – we *are* God – but not *we* as a multiple definition, but as a *singular* Being called God!

Does this then mean, as we begin to understand, that there will be no Soul in human form that will not recognise itself through the physical form? No it does not mean this, for time is immeasurable and this is why your world cannot end until all those from other worlds become One in the realisation of their true nature. Once a glimpse of this comes to the mind of man and those from other worlds, then will be the realisation that at this stage you are brothers, and brothers in recognition of their True-God-Self."

"Do you understand?"

The group remarked they could appreciate the necessity of patience being present in their spiritual progression and agreed they would endeavour to apply this valuable virtue.

Mark then posed the following question to Soren.

"Could you explain, Soren, how you access the future? Do you time-travel and do you have access to the Akashic Records for this purpose?"

"We project our minds into the future as do the workers of your Earth when they work clairvoyantly one to another, and you speak of future events. It is because in a child-like way you have projected *your* minds. As we have explained before, time in itself does not exist; therefore you as physical beings with the gifts of the physical being are able to move backward and forward in that which you call time.

In your dream state you can dream for what may seem a long period during which many events will happen in your sleep state, but when one looks at the clock all that has happened may have taken a very short time. This is because the mind has *total* freedom. The space in the mind takes on the attitude of a form recognised by you, the sleeper or the speaker, and you see what is to be. You are, in fact, drawing on that which you term the Akashic Records!

We have spoken of dreaming many times before to you Earth children, and you know the different depths of sleep, but man when he works in a clairvoyant state – and perhaps not consciously aware he is *in* that state – can sometimes see that which is ahead and see clearly but without understanding *what* he sees. This is why it is difficult for man to name a place or to give an exact date though this is what man desires. We of Spirit can go forward or backwards in time with total mind-control and because we can see clearly we can give definite details and information of the events, but again we can only say all things happen simultaneously because there *is* no measurement of time.

This has always confused man, for if what we see happens to man in ten years time, and *that* time does not exist, then how can we give a clear understanding? It is because man, simply because he *is* man, will insist on the time factor, but must wait till he passes through that time for that event to happen, but in truth it has *already* happened!

Time in measurement is at different speeds on different dimensions or levels. 'But', you say, 'I am in this dimension so how can this be?' All worlds interrelate and intermingle one with another, so the event that has been prophesised in man's life is already in action on that you would term the Astral Plane or different dimension, but it is not identical in the sense that man would understand. It is only as you progress onto the spiritual realms that you begin to understand true measurement.

So this will bring you an understanding of time travel as you say, because we as Spiritual Beings can project ourselves, as well as our minds, and reverse back to your time and you as speakers or dreamers can do the same thing and not age. Can it not be that everything happens simultaneously? How do you think we

come and converse with you in your time and yet remain in form, in our time? We project our thoughts to your *space* in time!"
"Do you understand what I am saying?"
Again the group thanked Soren and added that they knew their understanding was limited, but indeed would give further study of Soren's information.
Soren advised: "Read thoroughly when this is transcribed onto paper and if you dwell upon the words we speak in time - and I use the word loosely – you will understand that the information which we give now *will* eventually become clear to you because your minds are already capable of understanding our words. It is because you are thinking with the mind of a physical being influenced by the time factor of your world but you will eventually think with the mind of Soul-physical being and all will be clear."
"Thank you again, Soren, may I voice another question?"
This was said by Mark, who also remarked that Soren was an absolute gentleman, to which Soren replied with humour, "I know!"

The question related to Soren's world and he was asked would he expand upon the structure of his world, what they did on that world, and also how was their information obtained?
Soren continued good-humouredly, "How is it when you asked for one question to be answered, two or more manage to *slip* in!
Our information is gathered through physical lives. It is in our physical life upon yours and other worlds that we in a conscious state begin to seek that which is beyond our understanding, that which all men wish to understand, so therefore we grow on the Earth planes. When we return to the spiritual realms and become a conscious Soul without the hindrance of the physical body, all information and experiences including our emotional and mental states are in a Soul awareness, so we can begin to unthread the tangled mind of man with the clear mind of Soul. Information comes from within and we are educating ourselves to bring forth that which is already with man – which is already *within* you. As you are learning, so too did we, for there has always been contact with Spirit.
As to the structure of our world, it is as natural to us as your world is to you. We live as we explained, in a *'smoke-like'* form, but to us that form is not that. We to each other appear in a much

finer, but solid form. As you are, so too are we, but at different and finer levels of vibrations. We have our places of rest – of socialising, not as the man of Earth does, but a coming together in different groups of different centuries and from different levels, whereby we exchange and accumulate information and this is how those in the Realms of Spirit expand mentally and spiritually. We then return to a level of Earth with this knowledge and this information, and as we spoke of a few months ago, return as highly intelligent beings to your world and other worlds and our wisdom and our knowledge comes forth in a physical state at very tender years.

It is difficult to describe our world to a man of Earth who cannot see with the eye of the Soul. If, during your journeys to the astral realms under the guidance of your Soul-Self and if your mind could be cleared of the materialistic ways of your world, you would see our worlds as they are. But your understanding and your conscious way of thinking cannot envisage the way in which we live. We present to you that which is recognisable to you, i.e. a house is a house, but we do not live in houses. We are within what you may describe as temples, but they are *not* temples. They are places whereby the advanced mind and Soul progression gather in the Halls of Wisdom and the Universities of Wisdom and the places of music - the places of vision, the places of colour - and these are our homes. We do not live in a personal way as man does for we do not posses that form of personality. We possess an individuality which embraces all others. We recognise our One-ship.

Those who come to us from the Earth plane as young ones who passed from your world at a young age still continue to grow, but when they return to us, all that they knew before they lived in your world is remembered by the Soul mind, therefore that Soul continues its growth in a spiritual realm, but with a limited experience of earthly life. It is added to the knowledge the Soul has collected over many life times. Our world is totally natural to us, as yours is to you."

"Do you understand?"

The evening ended with the group thanking Soren for the talk and the information he has given them. He thanked them for listening and added there would be no more questions that night and said he would come again.

16

IMMORTALITY

"Very often man says and truly believes that he would not wish to be immortal – would not wish to live the life of the Immortals; and yet in truth that which dwells within him, the God Spark, the Spirit of Divinity and the Soul, of which man is the Caretaker, *is* Immortal, and he, himself is not! And yet man becomes distressed when he is told that he is to die and that it is simply the Soul that lives on and his body is put into the earth and no longer is, but simply becomes part of that which it once was and this is true. Of man there will be nothing! But within that Soul which has walked this plane with man will be all which that man has learned, all that he has gained and that he has experienced, whether it be pain or joy. This is a treasure to Spirit for it enables that Soul-Self to go forward with that added element of man; and man is immortal, but not in the physical sense which man wishes to be. For man in his limitations believes that he as he stands on this Earth, is the entirety of his True-Self, and this is not so. His entire self is the Self of the Soul and man is that through which the Soul experiences in the earthly realm.

Man is afraid of losing his identity and yet in truth his identity is that of the Soul. It is the personality which has been created on the physical plane that man identifies with and not his True-Self. We have said all through these chapters that man has separated himself from God, from Spirit, from his own true Self and the Soul that speaks. If man truly understood the way in which he casts from himself the coat of life – the physical body – then he would become joyous knowing that in his Freewill he has chosen to lead the life of the Soul, and in receiving this Soul element within his own physical form becomes part of that in a conscious Self; but because of man's impression of his own grandiose Self, he is reluctant to leave this 'coat of identity' from himself as he aspires to grow spiritually. But in his spiritual growth he begins to realise that it is only through physical form – in a physical world – that the Soul, which is an intricate part of him which in its identity *is* him but in itself is a part of God and Spirit, then man begins to understand the reason why he has been given Freewill. For in his short span of life upon the Earth he himself becomes a Spiritual Being in a conscious state of understanding and allows that spiritual God-Spirit-Soul to manifest.

The reason why man suffers is because of his denial of his True-Self. The reason why there is starvation and pain in your world is because man denies his True-Self. If he allowed that manifestation of his Soul with the Wisdom of which the Soul consists and the spiritual grandeur and joy and the manifestation of the True God, there would be no pain in your world and man would live a joyous existence!

It is man that prevents the manifestation of true Spirit. Man in his questioning asks 'Why then was the physical being created?' And we of Spirit would tell you the reason is because it is through the physical form and the world of God-Creation that God himself can experience, in its growing form of the Soul, all of that which he has created; so he chooses to live upon a physical world in a physical form to allow all pain and joy to be experienced in the God sense and as God, Spirit, Soul grows and begins to influence the mind of man, then pain will gradually diminish and eventually be erased from his Garden on Earth.

When man looks upon another who suffers in his world, he too suffers the pain because he is a being of compassion and yet it is only the pain of one who is connected by blood that creates the pain to the degree that is suffered. Man is not truly affected by the pain which is suffered by those of whom he knows nothing. It may be that a shadow of compassion will touch the heart, but he does not understand the true pain of suffering, therefore it is the choice of the Soul to enter a world of suffering, thereby strengthening the form in which it lives to overcome and be strengthened by pain. 'How', you may ask, 'can one be strengthened by pain?' When one looks upon another they love who suffers, they are strengthened by the intent to help and ease the pain of that one. This is why doctors and nurses of your world choose to become involved in this kind of work, so they may ease the suffering of others, but unfortunately the medical profession become entangled in the material rewards that can be drawn from the ones who suffer.

It is only when man, in union with Soul-Self, attends another who is suffering, will his own heart pain be lessened, for he is then at his own natural tendency of healing ability and can enjoy – through the eased pain of another – the Soul's joy of touching the heart of another Soul. He does not become satisfied with *his* ability to heal in union with Spirit, but becomes a man who is in *union* with Soul-Self, and rejoices at that healing *not* for self or man's satisfaction but for the God that is within, for God is perfect!

'If God is perfect why then is there suffering?' you may argue It is not God who causes one's suffering, it is the circumstances in which you live! It is the way you view suffering to be! Suffering is a moment's time in the development of the Soul manifestation and as you look back upon your time of suffering, you as growing spiritual-conscious beings will learn to appreciate your own strength and power in the physical sense; and as you grow in understanding of spiritual awareness, will come to the realisation that that power, that strength and that feeling of ability comes from the God that dwells within, the God of Perfection!

Then you ask, 'Why it is when I apply in a conscious effort to bring that healing to another who suffers, why do I fail and why is the result continued suffering? Or why is the result death, when I am trying to improve and lengthen that other's life?' You as individual, conscious, physical beings have come to that *conclusion* in the material way of thinking; it is not the Soul's way of thinking! The Soul in its growth of manifestation of its God-Self understands that each Soul aspect of man has chosen a particular path and if during that path a disability or death occurs, it is the choice of that individualised Soul – *that* Soul has made *that* choice!

So therefore, if you can understand that the true sense of healing is to awaken the Soul aspect into the conscious mind of man, *that* is the miracle which you, as an awakened Soul, is endeavouring to do! If the Soul is allowed to manifest amongst the sick and suffering and the dying of your world, that is sufficient and it will not be *until* man in true spiritual growth understands this miracle - although it may not be seen, but *is* experienced by the individual on whom he lays his hands - then it is of little value for the healers to continue!

There must be a spiritual understanding within you. You can ease each others' pain through comfort and you can ease each others pain through encouragement, but it is not until Souls touch and become united with the Spirit that is within all beings, and the true realisation of the God manifesting in all beings, will the World Soul be awakened.

When this World Soul is awakened it will not be in the individual way of thoughts – it will be in truth, a World Awakening not only amongst the physical beings, but the World itself; and the World will respond in its Spiritual growth and its accepted God-Self!

The World does not have the ability to think as man, it 'thinks' instinctively as a created world on its own creation and destruction and its reaction to man's abuse and the elements of its surroundings. It does not possess the sequential mind of man. It simply is! But as man recognises his True-Self and allows the manifesting of that Self, the world will respond as it would if the hand of God were laid upon it, for in truth, the hand of God is the hand of man!

You have been given Freewill to brush aside this power of God or to use it, but it is only through spiritual growth in the mind of man that will allow the true manifestation of your God World.

When we speak of immortality, it is to understand that all that you are as physical beings will always be, but in the Soul entity. Let us simplify this by saying to you: when you were a child there were memories imprinted in your mind that are with you now, but that child no longer exists, but it is an aspect of you in the form which you understand. When the Soul returns home you will no longer be, but all that you are will be retained in the Soul memory. So the child you were – the person you are, will always be! It is the Soul memory – your True-Self! You will not exist as the individual you recognise now when you return to Spirit as a Soul. All that you are now will be all that you will be *then*, for you are immortal! It is not until man begins to understand that his True-Self is the Soul-Self will he understand immortality.

Man has many lifetimes in which to delve and understand – to seek and absorb all that the Soul-Self truly is, and it is during these lifetimes, from primitive man to the man that he is now, and will be in further lifetimes, which will be brought forward into the Soul entity and man will begin to realise that as he passes to dust, he becomes immortal, the element of which you are as a physical being, part of the accumulation of the Soul wisdom. The Soul in itself is Wise, but you in physical form bring with the passing of your physical body the knowledge and experiences of the world and its adventures in life. For life is an adventure! Life is a joyous

experience for the Soul that is endeavouring to create within the mind of man the knowledge of his own immortality in the accumulation of experience, knowledge and Soul Wisdom!"
"Do you understand?"

The group thanked Soren, and Joseph, the leader of the group asked if there could be a question, to which Soren agreed and with his dry sense of humour continued at this point to state that when he agreed to one question, Mark, the prolific questioner of the group, managed to accumulate many questions in one sentence! Joseph said jokingly, "We thought you meant one after the other, Soren!" Amid laughter, a question was asked about a lecture both Joseph and Mark had attended recently and Mark stated he had intuitively 'picked up' that the speaker had emanated Light from himself and could Soren confirm and enlarge upon this?

Soren answered: "Light emanates from all living beings. The physical man emanates a Light Force that which you call the Auric Field, but the Auric Field around man – as we have said before – is dense. It is the light of the Soul that is within the physical form that manifests a true Light. If you mean you were aware of this emanation of Light this is so, but as you speak one to another there is always this vibration of a Light Force, but in one who is learned in spiritual matters it is accumulated in Spiritual Light and the growing Light within the physical form. In the union of the Light Force that emanates the manifestation comes the manifesting of man *and* his Soul's ability combined – Man and Soul becoming ONE!

Very often when one is in the presence of a Light Being who in himself is aware of that Light, there is a force that is manifested from that being and is physically felt by that other. That in its way is another Light Force. It is an energy that has physical repercussions on those that are around that one."
"Do you understand?"
"Yes, thank you Soren. With regard to what you said earlier, could you expand on what you meant by 'physical repercussions' please?"

Soren continued, "The physical repercussions from the advanced Light Worker – the one who has a knowing, in his own conscious mind – can create a moving force within himself. Very often they know this and often it will be repressed, but sometimes in recognising this he will allow this physical energy to go from his own physical body to others. It will not harm anyone, but sometimes it will create disturbing vibration sensations, but harmless in themselves, but to the observer the awareness is made.

Your world and ours consist of degrees of vibrations and with the Light Worker the vibrations are – although seeming dense to the observer – of such high frequency it literally cuts the vibrations of your world – the denser, heavier vibrations – and as this happens there is a break in the speed of these vibrations. Then the vibrations return to their usual speeds with which man is familiar. *This* change in frequencies is what man sometimes becomes aware of."

"Do you understand?"

"Are we saying then this is the force of Avartaric Energy?"

"Yes." Replied Soren. "There are many words to describe this energy and most of these words have been supplied by Spirit for man to understand, to visualise, to communicate and to recognise, one to another on all planes of existence. It is an energy used by the advanced Souls on the higher levels of the astral planes and above, the ones you refer to as the Hierarchy. Do not be coerced into believing there are only seven spiritual realms, for there are many, many more that man as yet does not have access to!

I simply prefer to use the description of finer vibrations which separates the heavier vibrations of the Earth, but it is created by the Avataric Energy. The result is the same!

"Do you understand?"

"So Joseph was right when he said his healing energies were uplifted after being close to this Light Worker?", said Mark.

"Yes, indeed, because from the Light Workers there will be an emanation of those same energies, and energy is energy! It is through Spiritual encouragement that comes from the Light Worker that creates the intensity of a lifted vibration around your speakers and healers, therefore the reaction of experiencing that finer vibration allows the Soul within that physical healer to manifest with more active energy through the healer towards his patient, for a pathway has been created through the denseness of the earthly vibration."

"Do you understand?"

"So it would be a permanent repercussion of being in that Light Worker's presence, then?"

"Yes," continued Soren. "It would be, but this vibration will eventually go from one to another as man grows spiritually. This then would lift the vibrations of your world and would be of benefit to your world and to man and the creatures that live upon it."

"Do you understand?"

"Yes, Soren we understand. Thank you."

Joseph at this point said, "Peace go with you, Soren," to which Soren replied, "Indeed, your peace be with me, and my peace be with you - bless you!"

17

QUESTIONS AND ANSWERS

"Tonight will be a night of questions but I will first broach to you a question, and we in Spirit who endeavour to teach the children of your world are often perplexed by the attitude of the young – and by young we mean the adults of your world – for the child believes in all that he is shown and taught, but with the adult there are always questions. He questions even his own truths and beliefs. The question I would ask this night is: What is it you have learned over these months? My question to you is: Do you feel you have a greater understanding of your Soul-Self in the realisation that you and Soul are one, and in that recognition of being one with Self do you also recognise the union with that which you call God? Do you have an understanding of what this God is?"

The small group of Joseph, Maureen and Mark looked at each other wondering which of them were to begin, which as usual resulted in Mark, the enthusiastic questioner, being the first to speak to Soren.

"Soren, I think you pre-empted me on this because prior to this evening I was going to ask if you could give an evening of answering questions, but initially may I say I thank you from the bottom of my heart for the information you have given us over the weeks we have spent in your company. I feel my understanding has taken quantum leaps forward and I know you and I jest considerably on this situation of my questions to you, but you must understand that when I have a fine teacher in front of me – as I see you and your group – the more questions I have and I'm sure you realise that, do you?"

Soren replied, "We of Spirit understand the questioning mind of the children of the world and you have asked the question that many of your people will ask and it is as yet the initial step towards your spiritual growth.

As is known many teachers use profound words which the ordinary man of the street does not understand and this is why he

114

draws away from the Spiritual Path for he feels inadequate; and yet the questions that are asked of Spirit can be answered in the most simplest way and this is what my group intends to do with the children of your world. It is hoped there will be another book and if not a book then a gathering of people such as yourselves, which will support and listen to the word of Spirit and in so doing come to an understanding of their own True Selves.

We have all walked your path and we have all had the inquisitive mind of man. We have all had the signs of doubt and of non-acceptance of this God which no-one can see – no-one can touch, and yet we have realised that though we may never see this God in the sense of seeing, we are at *one* with God – we *feel* with God. We are of the 'Waters of Life' in which this God dwells and this God consists of all that we are, but *not* in the sense of man's understanding and who *he* is, for he as man is of no great importance! This may seem upsetting for man to hear and yet as he grows spiritually he realises that he is *not* the man of Earth, he is Soul of that which you term heaven and man is a vehicle in which the Soul resides and man becomes *one* with his True-Self. This is what we have impressed upon you throughout this book – that man is *Soul,* is *Spirit,* and is *God*!

We of Spirit can not experience the Earth plane, its problems and its joys unless we reside in physical form and we have created that form in which we will live for a period of time on Earth. You as conscious beings have separated yourselves from us, thereby believing that when you die everything will die with you, but as we explained last week in the chapter of 'Immortality', this is not so. You will live forever in the form of Soul with the memories of what you once were, but that subject was covered last week to which you may refer – but tonight we invite your questions."

The following question was asked by Joseph, the leader of the group.

"Good evening, Soren. A little while ago you referred to new Souls coming to Earth and then carried on to say that they were not new Souls, that they are old Souls, but new to Earth. Can I ask where new Souls come from and what is the difference between old and new Souls? Is there such a thing as a new Soul?"

Soren's answer was, "There are no new Souls. The Soul has always existed for it is an aspect of God and God has always been.

A Soul is an aspect, a segment, a part of that Divine Entity you call God, and the Soul has always been!

The Soul not only experiences an earthly life in a physical form on your planet, it also visits other worlds and during its time on these other worlds remembers the experience it has under gone.

When we refer to the 'old' Soul it is one who through experience has gathered all the information that is of benefit to itself in whatever form it takes upon itself and in whichever world it is living. It learns quickly and adds to its Wisdom the knowledge of that other world plane, so therefore when it comes into another existence – and we will say an Earth existence – it comes with the ability to absorb and benefit from that existence of life. It learns its lessons appropriately and benefits by them.

The 'new' Soul has been in existence for as long as the 'old' Soul but nevertheless it has not gained by its experiences on the various levels of life for whatever reason and it is simply referred to as a 'new' Soul. But the ages of the Souls is exactly the same, for all Souls come from the same source. Do you understand?"

Maureen, the watcher of the group, then said, "Please, Soren, I would like to first thank you for the time you have graciously spent with us. Also for the care you have afforded us.

For me it has been a time of realization and at times I have felt humbled in the knowledge that I have been made aware of how little I have learned during my time on this Earth and of how much more there it to be learned in future lives. I have become aware and received a full understanding of God and the meaning of this word that we have given to the source of energy that we cannot always understand and through this energy and this name of God we do not always realise what role we have to play during our time on Mother Earth, and also the mystery of the beginning of life on this planet.

A problem came to my attention recently and perhaps you could help me to solve it – if there is a solution - that I may be able to give to a third party. You and your group are obviously aware of the situation to which I am referring." Maureen then went on to explain the situation. "Someone came to me and during the course of our talk she told me that if a certain conversation between two parties was disclosed to another Soul, party A. would put a curse on party B. The person who confided in me is already quite disturbed and now obviously more so. I tried to tell this person to

*return all negative responses with love for we are told love is by
far the strongest weapon on which we can draw. The one who had
threatened this curse also added that they worked on the Dark Side
and if anything of the conversation was repeated to another they
would take action. Soren, are you aware of such things on our
world and if so how would you deal with such matters and can we,
as Earth beings offer any help to this other Soul, who is obviously
very distressed?"*

Soren replied, "I cannot give you your solution for that has
to be searched for by yourselves, but the advice you gave was
good, but the question then arises – what is love and how does one
navigate that love towards an offender, towards one who
threatens? For man's love is governed by his material, his
emotional and his mental way of thinking and reacting to
situations. It is for you and that one and anyone to whom you offer
that advice to sit in the silence of your own being to allow that
love quality to emanate into your own heart-centre. Now we
understand the love of man, but it is to understand the love of the
Soul that is neglected in man's understanding. If, when you sit in
your silence, you bring to the heart a feeling of peace and
tranquillity and allow that heart-centre to expand and to absorb all
that is beautiful and as one absorbs the beauty of your world to
allow this experience to draw unto itself the love that you truly feel
for *yourself* – your *Soul* and your *God*, realising these things also
dwell in the heart of your enemy, and as you do this you will learn
to draw that love from your enemy and in so doing will direct it to
his conscious thinking mind and his materialistic heart. This is the
giving of true love to another. That other who works on the Dark
Side will not understand that this love was also drawn from him,
and his reaction to it will not be of a fearful nature but of a hesitant
nature, whereby his threat and his action will become weakened. It
takes great concentration on your part to emanate this God Love
from yourself but greater concentration is required to draw this
same love from one who works on the Dark Side. This then creates
a mirror of protection around you and the one with whom you are
concerned, but it also reflects not only the negativity back to that
one on the Dark Side, but the love aspect to that one. The result is
a state of confusion for a period of time. This state of confusion
will then allow those from Higher Planes to draw closer and to
magnify that God Love. It is not of a permanent nature because
man's heart is naturally selfish and wishes for his own desires to

be fulfilled, but if you and the one with whom you share this concern can sit in the state of allowing God Love to expand, it will lessen to a degree any threat that is aimed toward you. We of Spirit can work with the energy that love and hate create. We can transform these separate energies into one and because we work for the good of man the energy will be transformed into positive energy. This then can be directed to you and the one with whom you share the concern. In your world there are many dark energies at work as well as positive energies and this is leading to the eventuality of two Great Powers and it will be during the Aquarian Age when these two powers will surface; and these energies and these powers will be of the spiritual nature of light and the spiritual nature of the dark, for forget not that one who casts these negative energies towards you is also a spiritual being but without the realisation that true Soul is True Love.

The man in whom the Soul resides has temporarily crushed the desire of that other Soul and that Soul will need to return again in physical form. It is for you and your strength of Soul combined to manifest a greater aspect of love, but also for you to take into consideration the practicalities of life and actions needed to keep a distance from that one who threatens. It would be wise to give words of encouragement to the one who has been threatened, for that one to draw upon the aspect of his Soul-Self. You in your turn can only give as much as you possibly can and that is all that would be expected of you.

It pleases us to hear you say and use the word humility. It is a word not highly favoured by the man of Earth, for he believes it puts him into the category of a humble being in the eyes of man and one that is of true humility is raised higher than man for in humility lies true love, lies wisdom, lies great strength; so therefore sister, you are stepping on the Path of Spiritual Growth with an understanding that that which you give, you will receive. It may not be you will receive the joys of your world, but you will certainly receive the joys of Spirit connection between yourself and your Guide and the time will come for you when you will be a teacher amongst your own. Do not doubt your capability for all men are capable of wondrous things, whether it is word of mouth or action and in you is a natural tendency of gentleness of Spirit. You may at this point say there are times when you are angry and wish ill to another, and yet immediately – as once before – you govern this action of ill-feeling and your compassionate nature steps forward. Your Soul-Self is beginning to impress its true nature upon you. Do not doubt who you are!"

"Do you understand?"

"Yes, thank you, Soren," replied Maureen, "and you answered more than I realised I need to advance. You gave answers to questions I hadn't vocalised and I thank you for that and thanks also for the advice you have given for the party concerned."

"Soren, I understand the planes are divided into seven main levels and there are sub-levels also, would you expand upon this?" This question was asked by Mark.

Soren replied: "There are planes within planes. The seven Chakra Centres within your bodies are only a small number of the larger number that is within the physical body and so too, is it with the Seven Planes.

The Seven Planes, or different dimensions, in which man is so interested, are not separate Levels as one would see them. They are levels which intermingle and interrelate one with another as ours does now with *your* level of life. These levels contain and consist of a union of the physical forms in which the Souls reside which become – as you enter these different dimensions – finer or more gross bodies. We cannot describe in detail the beauties of these different levels of spiritual growth. We can describe to you the way of stillness and harmony which are in those Finer Dimensions and some of the men of the Earth level have heard the harmony of the music of Spirit. They have seen the colours which have been presented in their mind's eye, and of this beauty which consist of the world of Spirit.

As to the level on which my group and myself reside, as we have told you before, we come from a level that is a little higher than the levels with which you are familiar, but in so saying this, there is an accumulation of knowledge from these different aspects of levels, planes or dimensions. We do not live as you do, as we explained before. Our mind is exactly that – *OUR MIND!* And if you should separate *OUR* mind then the individual minds of my group would still consist of all the knowledge and information that is in *OUR* mind, for each mind is complete within itself. The reason we refer to our individual minds as *ONE* mind is because we *ARE* of one mind. Our thoughts, our understanding, our knowledge, our wisdom, our ability, our mental capacity are of equal standing, but as a united force of seven individual minds as *ONE* collective mind we are a greater force. The energy within our combined minds can assimilate fresh knowledge in moments and in being able to do this, can at this immediate time, separate and teach other groups simultaneously. Our words would not be as mine are to you this evening, our words would be separated and divided on the subject on which we speak. We can work with individual minds or with *ONE MIND!* We can also divide our *individual* minds to teach further classes on different subjects at the same time. This may seem difficult to understand, but the mind can divide and discuss and act upon different subjects simultaneously because we are growing towards a state of Pure Essence by which we have access to the minds of man and other beings of different worlds, different levels or dimensions. We are able to absorb, divide and teach separately as *ONE WHOLE* or as seven individual beings and there are still *further* divisions of these individuals!"

"Do you understand?"

Mark laughed and said, "Thank you, Soren, but again it is very difficult to assimilate that splitting of the mind!"

"No it is not!" replied Soren humorously. "For is that not what man did when he separated himself from that Divine Source? The difficulty is in realising and accepting the need to become *ONE* again with that Divinity. Man is on the road back to True Realisation of what he once was. It is man who makes the path difficult in his reluctance to become *ONE WITH THE MIND OF GOD!"*

Mark continued saying, "Well, I shall study the transcript when it is prepared – and study it yet again!"

"Good!" replied Soren, amid the laughter from the equally confused members of the group.

Further questions about the Akashic Records were then put to Soren, as to how they were read and who can view them. "Can you read mine right now?" asked Mark, "Would you expand upon this fascinating subject?"

"The Akashic Records have been given many names by different generations. It is a difficult subject to describe to you and is beyond the vocabulary of your world, but if you can envisage a hall that is constant in its size and is filled with light which shimmers, which resounds with the knowledge and wisdom of millions of years and of millions of lives and even the small thoughts of man, that is the Greater unconsciousness which we have access to. It is designed to a fashion similar to your ways of storing and seeking data, but it is done totally with the computer of the *mind*. If we wish to gain information of a life of an individual we simply tap into the identity of that subject. No man is exactly the same as another. Each one of you has a point of recognition which is your identification to those records, therefore, it is simply to know the identity of that individual and in so knowing can access further information which is required. But in saying this, it is not a careless action on the part of Spirit for if it were then it would be chaotic. There are those who govern this place of records. There are those who will not divulge the information if they do not deem it necessary for the advancement of the Soul that is seeking.

It does not mean that information is *not* available, it simply means, is it necessary to have? On the whole, as we have grown through the different levels of Spirit we have found that by studying man and Self and those on different levels and dimensions, we can understand the stories of their lives and the ultimate end of that physical life. We can through telepathy read the mind of an individual in whom we have an interest, but again, it is not an interest which simply erases our own boredom, or satisfies our inquisitiveness, for we do not suffer the state of boredom nor do we have the need to be inquisitive about others, but we use this information simply to help guide the Souls which dwell within physical forms, so the information we are allowed access to is also accessible to that Soul who because of its physical nature in which it dwells is not as clear as it would be if it were without form. So we can offer that information that is necessary for the Soul's earthly progress *if* it is *deemed* necessary, but that information is not *always* divulged to the human mind in which that Soul dwells.

As to could I "tap into" your records now – the answer is no, for it is not necessary. If you were truly aware of your Soul union and acted as one with Soul-Self and Soul-wisdom, your mental capacity would be able to access these records yourself in a conscious state of mind. But because man limits his ability to be at one with Soul, the Akashic Records remain inaccessible to him."

"Do you understand?"

"Yes," said Mark, *"but I do not wish to limit my relationship with my Soul. I firmly believe that information filters through to the conscious mind concerning previous incarnations and is often from the Soul-Self. Am I correct?"*

Soren then explained, "This knowledge can filter through, but if you are at *one* with your Soul at this precise time, you would not be attending this class. You would not be asking the questions you do, for you would know the answers. Not that a class of this kind would not of interest to you, but it would simply not be needed by you.

Man is his own teacher, and in being his own teacher is recognising his true relationship with Soul-Self in recognising his own Divinity.

Man separates himself from Soul. If man remembers a previous lifetime it is simply because there has been an opening in the conscious mind and this information is made accessible, but if you are at *one* with Soul-Self – and if I were addressing another Soul I would not need to use words, the thoughts that would be transmitted would be understood by your physical mind in Soul union and all knowledge would be open to you. If man had true accessibility to his Soul-Self there would be no need for us to work this earthly plane.

You are still a child on the road of discovery and if you have had a glimpse of past lives then that is of merit. Enjoy that which you perceive to be union with Soul for it will be before the end of your earthly existence that you will be more aware of your True-Self and your questions will then stop, for the answers will already be with you."

"Do you understand?"

"Thank you again Soren, and may I close this with something Socrates – who was one of our greatest thinkers – said 'the only thing I know is that I know nothing' and our conversations have certainly brought this forward to us. Very quickly before we close, you said you could access thought from us at any one time. Do you often do this with our group?"

Soren's quiet reply was, "Yes – but *only, only* if it causes you no distress knowing we do this. Your private thoughts remain private. Your private angers, hurts and joys are yours. We would not access your privacy unless it would be of benefit to you and with your permission – at least your Soul's permission!"

"Do you understand?"

Mark then said he could access Soren's mind at any time to which Soren quietly, humorously replied, "I don't think so!"

Amid laughter it was agreed that Soren often answered questions before they were asked and it was felt Soren was accessing the group's minds to which Soren said he was but also added that this was quite common practice with the Spirit teachers and went on to refer to the group's earthly childhood and the way in which they regarded their teachers as so knowledgeable, but as one out-grows each class in life one begins to look for a higher grade teacher and this the way of Spirit. "When we reach the Source of the Absolute do you think then the limitation will be ended?"

Mark admitted he was lost for words, but said the way Soren had spoken tonight was quite wonderful.

Maureen then said she was grateful also for these evenings and all the evenings Soren had spoken and on behalf of her colleagues and herself felt they were privileged and blessed at being present during these lessons of Soren's.

Joseph at this point, said, "We know this evening is coming to an end Soren, and we apologise for not answering your questions. I think, Soren, we are trying to blend with our Soul-Selves, but perhaps as yet we haven't fully understood totally all you have taught us about who and what God is, but as we read over the writing and listen to the tapes I'm sure our understanding will improve and be of benefit to us. As the others have said, and I can only repeat, thank you again for the evening. Bless you and Peace be with you, my friend."

Soren, in finishing said, "I will simply end with, as you have said, you are beginning to know yourselves and "Man know your Earth, and in so doing, know God" but I would leave you with these words, does one ever know oneself?"

Mark said quickly, "The man who conquers himself is the greatest warrior!"

Soren's quiet reply was, "Yes indeed, but the man who conquers *only* himself limits his ability!"

"Bless you and goodnight!"

18

AND AGAIN, WHAT IS WISDOM?

"Man does not understand what True Wisdom is and yet all of his earthly life he is practicing this art of seeking Wisdom and knowledge of all that is. The result of man's completion of this earthly realm should be that he passes into the world of Spirit with that which he left behind in the material plane, and what is this? It is simply accepting the true realisation of what he is, and it is through growth within the earthly existence that man begins to realise that his power and his glory is that which is manifested from within his Soul-Self – the aspect of Spirit – that small part of God – which resides within his physical form, but man persistently refuses to acknowledge this fact.

Man reads many books and listens to many speakers on the subject of Wisdom and in the profundity of the words uttered or read becomes confused, and yet the truth of Wisdom is a most simplistic task. Study the child of your earth and it is in learning the ways of man that the child is using the quality of Wisdom, and as the child learns he adapts that Wisdom into the materialistic view which was instilled into him from birth by his elders – man himself - and the child becomes a materialistic desirous being that wants only for himself. But already the children of Spirit are being born and are amongst you who will hold to *themselves* that True Wisdom. So therefore, where resides True Wisdom?

It is for man, as he learns the way of Spirit and as he watches those round and about turning to that which is beyond their understanding in a hope of true realization of the reason why they exist and from whence they came and to where they are going, that he begins to understand that the path can only be followed to its ultimate end. It is to the Heart Centre that man must now – at *this* time during the evolution of his world – *focus,* for it is within that centre that True Wisdom lies! The mind, if it has been disciplined, will co-operate with that which is within this Centre – and will be governed by that which is within the heart - and man's mind will become One with man's Heart Centre and with that which is in the Heart Centre – the Pure Essence of God

Love! Man has pulled a veil over this Love and made it his own - *his* love for the world – *his* love for another – *his* love for his own very dear physical life, takes priority over the Love of God! During the weeks we have spoken to you we have tried to instil in your minds the need of this discipline. The need to sit in the stillness and silence of your own being is absolutely necessary so you may take that Inward Path to the place of Divine Love. You have come from a time of materialism and you are entering into a time of spiritual growth that will not only blossom from the heart but take root in your minds and your minds begin to understand the Wisdom of the Heart and will follow patiently and loyally into that place of Stillness and Silence.

The Essence of God Love is beyond that which man has called his own and an idealism of his own ability to love. Man's love as we have said before is selfish. Man's love as we have said before is desire, but if man allows himself to take that inward journey – not to hear the voice of Spirit – not to see the beautiful impressions that are put upon his mind by Spirit – not to become aware of the music of Spirit or the colours and beauty that envelope him – but simply to enter the Realm of Purity – that realm of compassion, joy and love, then he will recognise his One-ship with God. He will recognise that he is not only *part* of the Divine but that he *is* the Divine!

Man, during this New Age that began before the turning of time, has come to realise he is on the Upward Journey and man has within himself the mentality of an intelligent being but with the animalistic nature of pure survival of creating that in which he can take pride. Pride has no place in the Heart of Peace, and it has no place in the Heart of Love. That Heart Centre, which is now beginning to expand and to manifest that Divinity of Love and Wisdom, is now taking its rightful place upon your world and man is coming from the place of selfishness – from the area known as the Solar Plexus which has governed man's actions and his desires over a very long period of time.

Man speaks of the different Root Races of the world and the majority of your world population is enmeshed in those Root Races of animalistic natures, but as you approach the Heart Centre of the Heart Race this is when man begins to become influenced by the Voice of the Soul, and when we speak of the Soul we mean that part of God which is within you – the Still Small Voice! "Love is where the heart is" and this does not mean a place to which your heart has been attracted, or to the place of physical birth, or of the physical heart delight, but the Heart Centre itself is the Home of Spirit and the Home of Love. So we would ask you if during these times when we have spoken to you of the various aspects and the abilities of man, have you as yet, come to the realisation that your journey is but a step away?

You speak of the astral levels within and without your world and which are within and without your physical bodies, and man longs to be where those he loves reside, but it may well be if your desire is so great that you *will* meet your loved ones on those levels, but also be aware that you may be disappointed, for in those levels there is an opportunity for spiritual progression, but not as great as it is on the earthly level as a physical being; for man, with his heart-governed consciousness, and his love aspect of God within him and also the ability to manifest in a consciously aware effort, the Love of God, will have reached beyond the lower astral planes when he returns to the world of Spirit!

Children of your world are now being born with this desire half-awakened within their physical minds and as they grow they will not seek to understand the Astral Dimensions, but they will seek to understand the mental and emotional levels of Spirit of which they are part. They have come *through* the realms of the astral planes to dwell among the children of Earth! You, as children much younger in your development than these children that are here and others who are coming, must be ready to teach, to guide, to encourage these little ones for they will be condemned and ridiculed by those of your world who are as yet, not seeking Self Realisation!

Again we must return to the Heart Centre. When you speak of love, when you experience love, it is from this heart area that the emotions are contained and yet when you learn of the way of Love of God through the manifestation of his Spirit and your Soul, you could not imagine the enormity of this Love but your ability *is* to allow this small rose of Love that glimmers in your Heart Centres to manifest itself to every fibre of your being. As you learn to do this and it becomes natural for you to do so, this love will then expand beyond your physical being. This is the Light and True Realisation, and your minds will be consciously aware of your capabilities. Your minds will be aware of the Love manifesting from the heart and the mind will be governed by that Heart Power!

If during our time together you have learned this simple truth in itself, and yet the hardest lesson for man to learn, then your knowledge and Wisdom of the mind has expanded enormously, which in itself will absorb the mind fields of others and you in your turn will be able to pacify the fear in others. It is for you to initiate that Love manifestation. At first it comes to you in small lights of understanding and in a little comfort and a minute form of joy which to you may seem to be of such greatness, but as you reach beyond in this conscious effort of realisation of the growth of that Love aspect and that Blazing Fire within, then this you will be able to manifest one to another without the necessity of the spoken word. Man will recognise his Soul-Self and in acknowledging the Soul-Self in another in a physical form, and as this love grows and manifests throughout your world, so too will your world respond, for it too is a growing conscious Being.

Within your world are thought forms which create the growth of your world, but these thought forms are governed only by the growth and the protection of the world. It – the world – is not governed by selfish thoughts, as is man, but it is rebelling in defence of Itself. There are many upheavals in your world and there will be more because man has created the assault upon his world and the world in its turn affects the Universe around it. The Universe echoes these assaults from one planet to another and the response from these others worlds and these other planets will be of a defensive mechanism, so therefore chaos will be! But as the beings of your world begin to recognise that the Love aspect has power over all things, and you learn appreciation of the value of your own world and the surrounding planets for your own physical survival, then you will begin to practice this Power of Love and eventually, as you grow spiritually, will come the Peace of mind for which man has craved for so long, and he will have found the solution of all things by connecting with the Heart Centre, and the joy of World Peace and planetary response will be! The Universe in which your planets are will become calm as the vibrations of Love extends from one world to another. Other worlds are also working towards this, and as you all progress on this same Path of Spiritual Wisdom, the time will come when your world will become involved with these other worlds.

But human beings are in the earthly stages of spiritual development of giving of this love because first *you* must experience the Divine Entity in you, and initially it may seem foreign to you and it may seem that this Love is being imprinted upon your heart, but this Love is that which is growing within you. This Love is that with which you came into your world. Call it God – call it what you will – but it is the power of this force which will discipline the aggravation of mind control. As has been said before, the mind is a 'chattering monkey' and it will try to draw your attention away from your states of stillness, and it will only be during your short time of Love Experience through which the mind will be overcome by the Peace and Tranquillity that enters it and it will become still. But the time will come again and again when you will need to practice control over this busy mind – this 'chattering monkey' within your being, that it may submit itself to that Divine Love from which you were created. For what is man's mind but Freewill? And what will it learn by entering the place of Stillness and Silence in the Heart Centre? It will submit to the Will of God and it will begin to understand the Wisdom it has so long craved for. The Book of Wisdom is in the Heart Centre and the mind begins to realise this truth!

You may ask, 'If I am created by Divine Love then why is not every aspect of my Being perfect?' and we would tell you every aspect of your Being *is* perfect! It is simply clouded by that which you see as *imperfect*. You are all as you are meant to be. Once you gain control over the busy, excitable mind and all the manifestation of True Love within that centre, you are beginning to expand, absorb and heal. All forms of illnesses, disease and disfigurement will be annihilated by this Love for Love in itself is *perfection* of all things including matter.

As this Love slowly blossoms within your Heart-Centre you are then approaching a world of new growth. You have crossed the time barrier between the manifestation of self-gain to the manifestation and glorification of Soul-conquering man! Now this does not mean man himself will become as nothing, for man is already nothing, but he is a being of conscious thought and the conscious thought is Love. When the Soul Love truly manifests in the heart of man and man recognises this is so, then it is the Soul which has become victorious and the union – when it resides within the conscious thought of man - becomes manifest on your earthly plane and God walks your Earth!

There are a few in your world who are born with a conscious realisation of what they truly are. They come as ambassadors in a conscious state of mind from the world of Spirit, recognising their true identity and their love and they are able to manifest this so it becomes recognisable by those of a less understanding. But in this understanding also comes the realisation that all this Love is simply laying dormant in *all* physical beings.

You speak of your downward journey from when you were once stone, or of the insect world, fish, animal and so forth, but within that stone and all those levels of growth that followed, is this Seed of Love. If it were not so, there would be no progression on the Earthly Plane and even as you reach a level of physical man this Seed is still in the darkness of the Heart Centre and is governed by the mind of man. But it is already beginning that this Seed of Love is starting to blossom and as it does – as it struggles to the surface of man's mind - comes the *understanding* in man's mind that within the heart lies all Wisdom; and the seeking mind will find this Wisdom and when it does and succumbs to that Wisdom, the knowledge of Spirit which will enter the mind in true understanding will manifest and man will grow to his true potential and his true perfection, for it is through this understanding that man will endeavour to perfect humankind.

There will be no pain in your world –

This will not be in your time –

There will be no sorrow in your world –

This will not be in your time –

These words I address to the group present this night. You will continue your lives in this world of suffering, for it is man himself who has created this suffering by allowing his mind to maintain control over the Heart of Wisdom! Within you is that glimmer of Love to which your conscious minds are becoming familiar and as you reflect in this beauty which is there, you are helping to pass this message one to another in your world and this glimmer will eventually become a blazing light. There will be no need for man to communicate with words, for another will see this natural beauty of the Soul Love and will respond to it!

You at present are beginning to respond to that little love which is sleeping in your heart. It is slumbering until your mind - in total submission to the beauty which is within, relinquishes its power, and it is for you - the Soul - to use your ability to help subdue the mind!

Who do you think creates your discipline? Who do you think helps you on your homeward journey? It is both you and your Soul for you are One, and the closure of man's journey will be when the mind in total submission and acceptance of its True-Self realises this.

Once you allow that Heart Centre to manifest this Divine Love, the mind in its growing consciousness will realise the great part is has played in allowing the strength of the Soul, that is in physical form, and is Divine Love, to conquer those desires and wants of the material plane. You will see the treasures returned to you for they have never left you. They have been hidden in the Heart Centre of your Soul physical body.

Love is simple, wisdom is simple, it is man who makes the journey difficult for he constantly searches outwardly for the miracles of Spirit to be presented to him.

The miracles of Spirit are within him -

For he is Spirit -

For he is God!

Albeit an aspect -

Albeit a tiny glimmer -

And if God is Love,

Then so too, is Spirit –

Is Soul –

Is Man!

When this realisation in the union of the Love in the heart imprints itself in its true form, in the mind of man, then man himself will recognise his own splendour as the harbinger of God's word to the people of the world. God will be made manifest again and again and again!

It is hoped that as each of our groups in the world of Spirit come to the children of your world, at least one of you will be awakened to this Truth and when you think of the numbers of group gatherings such as this in your world being activated at this precise moment, then how many of you are being awakened to your true potential?

It is in all forms of life that these groups are gathering together. It is in all forms of rich and poor that this understanding is being given and if only one of you in each group is aware of this understanding that all Love and Wisdom dwells in the Heart. then imagine the word of God being passed from one to another. Wisdom, Love and Compassion dwell in your heart – awaken to this knowledge. Still your mind and make your path clear and smooth as you step into this splendour of Spirit and the Blazing Light of understanding and the Burning Fire of Love will cleanse away all selfish desires and wants and you will become a Perfected Man of Earth knowing other Perfected Beings are happening NOW!

It is the time of mental realisation!

It is the time of emotional control!

It is time to open the door of your Heart!

The prophets have knocked upon these doors for aeons of time. Open the doors of your Hearts and allow the prophets, seers and all who come to be with you.

Blend your Souls!

Magnify the Spirit!

And manifest God!

Do you understand?"

The group thanked Soren for his wise words and Joseph remarked that it takes a long time for this understanding to be absorbed to which Soren remarked:

"But as you look back and draw to your mind the knowledge you have learned from others, and the realisation of all your frantic endeavours to grow spiritually dawns upon you that it is such a simple step to take - to be still and at one with yourself. It takes many, many lifetimes for this realisation to come to man, but it is *this* lifetime in which this will be!"

Soren then agreed with the group that there would be time for questions but at first went on to say: "Yes, there is time, but our time together is now short as we come to the close of this book for now there will be work for this one (referring to Melsa) in collating these chapters we have shared."

"Soren, may I thank you again for that fine teaching and since we last met I have listened again to your tapes and read the transcripts. My question to you relates to myself as one who wishes to drag myself up from zero knowledge of the Spiritual Planes to a God-realised entity, but indeed I now understand why you refer to us as children. Could you explain how we could accelerate ourselves through the various planes of evolution to your level of consciousness"? This question came from Mark.

"There is in your world a story that is told to children about "The Hare and the Tortoise;" replied Soren. "It is wise to be the tortoise! So although it may seem to you that you are making slow progress it is because you are absorbing all that there is to absorb in your life of study and understanding. So therefore, the journey you make will not come to completion for many more lifetimes. You *cannot* accelerate your speed to reach a certain level. You *can* go beyond *certain* levels of the astral planes and this is simply because in the conscious plane in which you dwell now you have absorbed a great deal of spiritual knowledge. This enables you to pass through that first level which is described as the Summerland, but it may be that in your hearts – of selfish hearts – you may wish to meet again those who have gone before, your loved ones, and if this journey is desired then your progression in spiritual wisdom would be enhanced, but it may also be tinged with the regret of not touching that level in which those you love have chosen to stay for a period of time. It depends on how detached you are able to become from earthly desires, for those who have gone before are part of that earthly desire. So the way of the tortoise, in truth, is the wisest way. That does not mean your spiritual growth will be lessened or delayed, it simply means you will complete the course of returning home on *every* step of the way. But if you desire to accelerate your spiritual growth, this can be done on this level of Earth. The mind, under the governing of the heart, is able to absorb great spiritual knowledge and as it gains this knowledge it must grow to a degree of understanding that the heart takes precedence with the Wisdom of this knowledge, the combination of both being an asset to the man in physical form. The 'way of the tortoise' can bring great speed to man's spiritual growth, but the way of the tortoise covers all aspects of life. The hare in his flight to reach the goal post could miss an understanding of Wisdom and therefore his journey would have to begin again!"

"Do you understand"?

"Yes," replied Mark, "I understand about "The Hare and the Tortoise" but a great difficulty I have is a burning within me for Spiritual knowledge which would drive me forward and yet I must accept the fact of being the tortoise, but it is coming to that point of balance. Can you understand where I'm coming from, Soren?

"Yes" said Soren, with humour in his answer. "But also the Tortoise can run if it so chooses!"

Mark laughingly remarked, "Your point is taken, Soren, thank you."

Joseph asked the next question which was based on the belief of many that the life we live at present is an illusion and could Soren explain what is meant by this expression.

Soren's answer was: "The world itself is *not* an illusion. Man and all he sees is *not* an illusion. What *is* an illusion is the way in which man's mind *perceives* life to be, that creates the illusion. You speak of the devastation that is happening in your world and this is an illusion of the mind. The devastation which is happening *must* happen for the world to become as it is intended to be - that of beauty! The dark time which is around man now is an illusion of devastation in man's understanding of spiritual progression. That which *needs* to go *must* go and the world is erupting and clearing itself of these negativities. This is the truth behind the illusion. Man sees himself as the greatest creation of God. *This* is an illusion. Man within whom the Soul resides is the *greatest* creation. This is *not* an illusion – this is *fact!*

It is man's way of seeing and understanding the world and its people that is the illusion. As you look through a candle light it will distort that which is beyond because of the flickering of the candle, and this is how man sees his fellow brother and the world in which he resides. *This* is how man sees the Glory of God, but he cannot see clearly. He has created his own illusion. We of Spirit try to clear the debris from your seeing and your thinking, but man prefers to create that curtain of dusk-like vision rather than look with the eye of spirit. Your world is following the design of the pattern of God and it is turning in its return journey. The out-breath is finishing and the in-breath is beginning!

That which you see and feel and hear is real, but it is how man perceives things to be that creates the illusion in his thinking mind, because all men's minds go in different directions and that which he sees brings a wrong perspective to his way of thinking. So the illusion originates from man's mind. That which is, *is* – that which is not is created by man's fear and reluctance to accept the changes that are occurring and must be for the vision to be cleared and for man to see that which is real!"

"Do you understand?"

The group thanked Soren again and agreed they understood. Soren then went on to say his farewells.

"It is now time for me to go and I thank you, and we from Spirit appreciate that you have allowed us to come and speak to you and it is hoped we have helped you on your journey. It is also hoped by us who have walked with this one for many, many years, that we will again be invited to work through her so that we may, through groups such as this, become one. And when this happens it is hoped that you three will have become familiar with teachers who are simply waiting beyond the doors of your hearts and minds. It has brought us great spiritual delight to work with you.

We thank you and we bless you."

Amid the murmured thanks and blessings from the group, Soren left us.

SOREN'S ADDRESS

"I would now address this small group who have been so supportive to our cause, who have absorbed that which we of Spirit have come to inform you and it has pleased us that your response and attendance at these quiet evenings have been such a delight to us. Not only to hear those of us who have on occasions taken turns to speak, and yet we speak as one, but to perhaps answer the questions in each of your minds and these questions are 'Who am I?', 'What am I?' and we would tell you this: You are vehicles of the Soul! You have an identity which is known to you as your personality and it is more often than not that your personality overrides your true identity, but your Soul is your true identity and its desire is to manifest the True Self and in so doing manifest the Spirit and that of God.

As man begins his journey in this life or other lives, he begins to realize that that which he knows in this life was also there in his previous lives, but with the added knowledge of this and other lives, so therefore man must grow – even though unconsciously – and he will grow until he becomes familiar with the Soul aspect. He will begin to acknowledge that without that breath of God he cannot be, and in understanding this will, in truth, identify himself with God *as* God, but not in the personal manner of the little 'I am', but in the acknowledged individual of the great 'I AM'; and man in becoming one with Soul will walk in future lives manifesting that which you identify as God, but in the Glory that man at this stage of his spiritual evolution cannot imagine.

If I spoke to you as separate personalities you would identify yourself by your name, by your profession, by your family and those with whom you are familiar, but would it be the true Self that is endeavouring to manifest through you, the physical form? There are times momentarily, when the mind of each of you becomes overwhelmed with the awareness of not being you, the personality, and it is at these times that the identity of the Soul begins to project itself. As you become more familiar with the identity of the Soul - and it will be a gradual process - you will cast

135

aside the will of man and identify only with the will of God in recognising your true status as that of Soul.

You will no longer be drawn to personal desires. Your desire will be to allow that manifestation of Soul, of Spirit, and of God and this will be your true identity. In recognizing your true individual identity you will then progress to embrace all that is, and become part of everything and everyone in a conscious manner. The personality will no longer be, but will become as a shadow of your past lives. The time will come when you will recollect past lives, and as you do you will begin to realize that as you grow from childhood to adulthood in this world, and your previous lives when you were once a child and reaching adulthood through many lifetimes, that you have gained another growth with the knowledge of your mind.

This knowledge comes from the heart – the home of the Soul – and it is in the stillness of your being that you identify yourself with Soul. You are no longer the one known by a name, a profession or a position but you begin to be part of all things. At times during your true meditation, when you reach that place of oneness, when you reach that place of being one with all things, then that time will come in a *conscious* manner in the mind that reflects on its true identity – the true Self!

At the present time, in your world man is too busy to BE, yet we of the spirit world would ask you simply to BE and in that BEING the realization of your BECOMING will enter the conscious thinking mind. There will be times when your mind is filled with darkness and your heart heavy and it is during these times that you should strive to become one with Soul and if you can reach this mind-state of total awareness of true Self, the heaviness and darkness will no longer be, for you as physical beings will be bathed in the light of spirit. You will reflect back that which you truly are – your identity – *not* the personality, which will be cast away like a shadow by the beauty of the sun, but the true identity of your spiritual Self becomes apparent.

You speak of the problems in your lives and you allow these problems to take priority over your spiritual growth and in so doing you feel you are delaying that growth, and yet in truth, you are experiencing a worldly life whereby all the happenings will be rained upon you, be they good or bad. You will begin to realize that no matter how heavy the rain falls upon the physical body and mind, it cannot darken the light that dwells within, and *you* are that light!

I address both man and Soul and in this union of your being One, you will begin to understand the story we tell you, for this story is as old as life itself and life itself has always been in the form of that which you term as God, for he is life. Those of you whom you speak of as Spirit and the Souls in your animal kingdom – your angelic world and in the world of darkness, then this light of knowledge must eventually be and the world of darkness will gradually awaken to this light, as those on this level of Earth are beginning to do.

There are many such as yourselves who cannot as yet express the Divinity that dwells within you. You cannot put into words the joy you feel during those moments of stillness, but that joy is sometimes weighed against the problems of your world which often eliminates the joy that once dwelled in the conscious mind and heart. You must constantly seek within during your still and silent times in your meditative states and seek only the bliss of God – seek only for the compassion that your Soul feels for you, its physical form, and be comforted by it. Be aware of the greatness that you carry within you and that greatness will appreciate your cooperation in two minds becoming ONE. Man's mind and Soul mind."

After a brief period of silence Soren continued with humour in his comment,

"And is this when I ask, 'Have you all gone home?'"

The group laughed at Soren's remark and Joseph went on to ask if there could be questions. Soren agreed and Mark as usual was the first to begin.

"Thank you again Soren, for coming to speak to us and for the effort you have put in during these months and we thank you from the bottom of our hearts for the time we have spent together in your company of friends."

Joseph then asked Soren if he wished to add anything more to the evening's address, to which Soren replied.

"Simply to comment we are very much surprised to have not been asked anything in particular from our inquisitive young friend tonight"

Amid laughter and banter from the group, and as Mark made to reply, Soren continued:

"But perhaps it is because his mind is so full of questions that he does not know which one to ask, or perhaps it is that he is beginning to realize that the questions he has have already been answered and sometimes he suspects this! And we would ask you to understand that there are times when an answer comes before the question, but do not suppose that these answers are coming from the mind that is learned or the mind that has read many, many books or to the one who has attended many lectures given by others, but it is under the direction of your Soul-Self that is supplying many of your answers. Do you understand?"

The group murmured their agreement and then Mark went on to state, "Soren, may I refer to a previous meeting, when you said...", and again Soren interrupted with, "Ah, I knew this lack of questions would not last!"

"Yes, we were wondering where Mark's questions were too!" laughed Joseph.

Mark continued amidst the laughter. "I have a multiplicity of questions, Soren, to throw at you and I can only say that you have pushed me forward massively and my understanding has expanded so hugely that I can only thank you again, but hopefully at another meeting, I assure you I will be well-prepared to throw so many questions at you that I'll 'throw you backwards on that one!" to which Soren murmured, "Sufficient to say 'ah'!"

Mark went on to add, "I will catch you up eventually, Soren, and I have said this before!"

Soren continued, "It is hoped all beings will 'catch up', but no-one *can* 'catch up'. One reaches various levels in their physical way of thinking and it is not until the questions are no *longer* asked when man begins to develop his own true wisdom. This wisdom being given to him by Soul-Self which man absorbs as truth *without* question. He becomes the one who waits and in waiting all answers *are!* But man is in the School of Life and in the School of Life all questions are constant. In the School of the Soul questions are not needed, for answers are already there and the advanced Soul knows this.

Now, when I say 'advanced Souls', I am not saying Souls are not equal – what I *am* saying is the Soul which walks in physical form at times, becomes weary of *being* in the physical body and in so being can become saddened by what it may feel is a delay in the progression of man - *not* Soul - and it is sometimes the Soul that dwells in physical form that will question those of us on another dimension as to how to progress and persevere to infiltrate man's mind. So the questions Soul asks are simply how to encourage the body in which it dwells to grow spiritually, to bring forth the true manifestation of God, which the Soul is eager to do through the form of man on an earthly plane."

"Do you understand?"

Once more the small group of friends thanked Soren for his wise words and agreed the time had come to end the evening's talk and Joseph closed the meeting with, "May God's Light and Peace be with us."